Stories that Heal

Stories that Heal

MICHAEL BUCKLEY

daybreak

London

First published in 1989 by
Daybreak
Darton, Longman and Todd Ltd
89 Lillie Road, London SW6 1UD

British Library Cataloguing in Publication Data

Buckley, Michael
  Stories that heal.
  1. Christian life
  I. Title
  248.4

ISBN 0–232–51841–6

Most of the Scripture quotations are based on *The Jerusalem Bible* published and copyright 1966, 1967 and 1968 by Darton, Longman and Todd Ltd and Doubleday and Co Inc.

Phototypeset by Input Typesetting Ltd,
London SW19 8DR
Printed and bound in Great Britain by
Courier International Ltd, Tiptree, Essex

Contents

Introduction

I like stories. I always have done. My father was a born storyteller. It was part of the Irish in him. As children we sat enthralled for hours, night after night, in front of the fire, as he told stories of his own childhood, and of the people he met who had an influence on his life, making him the kind of person he was. It didn't matter if they were famous politicians like Parnell or Julia Murphy, the shop-keeper at the corner of the street. My father knew them and we saw them through his eyes.

The people he talked about were part of his life, and because he meant so much to us they were part of our lives too. They became real people to us, as if we had met them ourselves. He made them come alive as he re-lived his own experiences with us. Time and again we asked him to tell us once more about someone or something that meant a lot to him. He never refused. No matter how many times he told the same story it never lost its magic, its appeal. All the stories were compelling listening because they were true, and we were being told them first-hand by someone we loved and who loved us.

In 'Pause for Thought' a lot of what kind of person my father was rubs off on me. Just as storytelling was very important to him as a special way of communicating things he held precious in his life, so my talks on the Derek Jameson show are very personal to me. It is as if I am sharing something that is part of me with one or two close friends. It is communicating something very deep inside me, with my friends, in the hope that it may find an echo in their lives and experience.

People whom I write about in *Stories that Heal* would be amazed if I were to tell them what passed over from their lives to mine. Some are famous, like Mother Teresa of Calcutta, others are as ordinary as John, our community gardener, while others, like the hippie on the London train who changed my attitude to young people, must remain nameless because we never got round to saying who we were. The one thing they all have in common is that they touched and influenced my life. I am today what countless people have made me because of the kind of persons they were.

None of us is an island. We need the help and healing of others so that we may grow as persons. I believe that nothing happens by chance, and that in our journey through life there is no such thing as a chance meeting with our fellow pilgrims. People are sent across our path, and it is important that we take each encounter and treat it as sensitively as a rose. Perhaps it will only be later, on reflection, that we will become aware of its significance in our lives. As a rule these encounters do not make a great show of themselves. They are ordinary, everyday happenings whose secret, hidden healing power is discovered only if we give ourselves time and space to read the message.

Jesus was a great storyteller. His stories were taken from life, and gave life to those of his listeners who applied them to themselves. His life-style gave the edge to his stories. It was the cutting-point. His stories healed because they touched people's minds and hearts. In some little way I pray that the stories in this book may be healing stories. If you see yourself in any story then you and I have met in that person. Through that person we have both been healed.

Dedication

**To my father
whose stories will always live
in my memory**

Jealousy

If you remember at the altar that your brother has something against you, go and be reconciled with your brother first, and then come back and present your offering. (Matthew 5:23)

We all want inner peace, peace of mind and heart. To be able to live out each day completely free from tension and anxiety. And yet it is difficult to find this peace in our crazy, noisy world. We may start off the day with a song in our hearts, and a firm resolution to remain at peace, but before very long someone or something throws us off balance. It is terrible if the cause of our disturbance is close to us, someone or something we just cannot avoid. What do we do then?

Joe is a perfect illustration of what I mean. He was a very successful architect with a loving wife, Elizabeth, and two happy, healthy children. His business was expanding so rapidly that he went into partnership with David. At first everything was flourishing with David, both in the growth of their business and in their personal relationship. They were real buddies. But Joe began to notice that David was becoming more in demand with their clients. Jealousy set in, and David got right under Joe's skin. Petty arguments became the order of the day, and gradually their office became a hell on earth with divided loyalties among the staff.

Joe's family life suffered most of all. He hardly ever spoke kindly to his wife and children, or took them out for a meal, or had fun with them. Their family life was dead. Then Joe developed what seemed like arthritis in his right hand, and was forced to take a month's leave for treatment. At home he was like a caged lion.

One evening Elizabeth sent me an urgent call to come and visit their home. I spoke with Joe, and he poured out all his bitterness towards his partner David, his wife Elizabeth and his family. Everyone was wrong except himself. Eventually when the tirade died down I talked to him about the past, and how peaceful he used to be. Didn't he want to be the same now? 'Oh yes,' he said, 'but how?' 'Get rid of your jealousy of David,' I said, 'and you will see everything fit into place.' He looked angrily at me at first, and then when I prayed gently with him, he said, 'Yes. What do you want me to do?' 'Write a letter of reconciliation to David,' I said. 'But I can't,' he replied quickly, 'I haven't been able to hold a pen in my hands for months.' 'You will now,' I said, 'when you write that letter.' He sat down at his desk and as he wrote his sincere letter of sorrow all his petty jealousies left him. But more than that, his hand lost its arthritic pain, and a look of peace came over his face.

2

Today his family are very, very happy indeed. Joe has put them before his business. His work has become a joy again, and the arthritis which threatened his livelihood has disappeared. Jealousy is a very destructive force. It cripples our ability to love. It was the jealousy of the Pharisees which was the root cause of their desire to put an end to Jesus. He was their enemy. Jesus said we were to love our enemies, and forgive them. Love casts out jealousy. When we forgive, then we will know deep inner peace, a peace that no person or thing will ever destroy.

Father, you have called us to live together in this world as friends; may we share, encourage and rejoice in the gifts which you have given to others so that the darkness of jealousy never clouds our minds and stops us acknowledging that every gift comes from you who are the Father of all.

Power and Happiness

Jesus went down with Mary and Joseph to Nazareth and lived there. He increased in wisdom, in stature, and in favour with God and men. (Luke 2:51–52)

Tom's story has a message for many of us. Soon after I met him I felt that the world was his for the taking. He loved life and lived it to the full. He fell in love with, and married, Betty, an equally outgoing person. When I officiated at their wedding, I sensed that here was the perfect partnership. Early on in their marriage they lost a baby daughter suddenly through some mysterious virus, and I was amazed at how well they supported each other then. But they were blessed with three other beautiful children, and it was one of my great joys to visit their home.

Tom did extremely well in his business career, but he never allowed it to interfere with his home life. Betty and the children always came first with him. He spent practically all his free time with them. But then he was offered promotion which he felt he could not refuse. It involved him in business trips to Europe which meant he had to

4

spend a great deal of time away from home. By a gradual process of erosion, business took over his life, and even though still a very good family man, things had changed at home. So had Tom.

He sought me out for advice. 'I don't know what is happening to me,' he said. 'Betty and I seem to have drifted apart. It's not her fault, she is a family woman. But she doesn't seem to understand what terrific pressures I face in my business. I work every hour that God sends, and when I come home I just want to flop down in an easy chair and forget about everything. But work follows me home because the phone never stops ringing. Betty and I never seem to relax in each other's company any more, and all the joy seems to have gone out of my life. What do you think I should do?'

We talked well into the night. Tom read the signs correctly, and it was up to him to decide what to do with his life. Eventually he had the rare courage, and loving support of his wife Betty, to make the decision to step sideways out of the promotion race. His business associates thought he was foolish throwing away such a marvellous opportunity. The last time I saw him he was much more at peace within himself and more mature in his attitude to life. There was laughter in his voice and for him, Betty and his family, life was again really worth living.

I know it isn't easy to make decisions like Tom's, but he didn't make it alone. As well as Betty, he had a very deep Christian faith which told him that the most important thing in life was

5

to be happy doing what God wanted him to do. He remembered the words of Jesus, 'What is the point of gaining the whole world, and in the process losing yourself?' So perhaps we might take a look at ourselves and our style of life. Are we under pressure to succeed? Wouldn't we be freer, more at ease with ourselves and those we love, if we allowed ourselves more time and space in which to relax and do the things we really want to do? You and I have to decide what we want from life. Once we have decided, we need the courage of our Christian faith to see it through. Then we will really be ourselves and be happy.

Father, your Son Jesus taught us the value of family life, and the need to have a true balance and sense of values so that we may grow in inner peace and in our personal relationships with those around us; may we, inspired by his love and grace, never lose our sense of priorities and find the courage necessary to lead a truly loving Christian life.

The Healing Community

The whole group of believers was united, heart and soul. The apostles continued to testify to the resurrection of the Lord Jesus with great power. (Acts 4:32–33)

I want to tell you about Maria. It is a wonderful story. A story of caring and sharing by her family and those round her. A story of healing through love and prayer which gives us all a message of hope.

The story began on Friday, December 18th, 1987. Maria was doing her last-minute Christmas shopping for her family and friends when she was knocked down by a van and cruelly injured. She had very severe head injuries, and her right shoulder and arm were so smashed that at the hospital the authorities said she would never be able to use them again. She was in a deep coma for several weeks, and on a life-support machine for seventy-two hours. She received excellent attention from the nursing staff. As she lay in a deep coma her parents, by her bedside, held her hand, played tapes, constantly talked to her and encouraged her to live. From Maria there was no

7

response. Her parish priest, Fr Peter, despite his other heavy parish duties, visited her every day.

Christmas time in Maria's home was a lonely and anxious one for her parents and two brothers, Martin and Patrick. Then came a very heavy blow. On New Year's Eve the consultant told Maria's parents that there was nothing more they could do for her. The parents had to be prepared for the fact that Maria could be hospitalized for the rest of her life, with her right side paralyzed. It was at this time that our healing group was contacted, and we said Masses and prayers for Maria's recovery. We went to London on January 28th and there we met and prayed with Maria's parents, Mary and Martin. It was their dearest wish that Maria would speak to them. We prayed that she would come out of her coma. As they went off to hospital to be with their daughter we asked our congregation of about eight hundred, who had come together for a healing Mass, to pray that Maria would recover consciousness and that her speech would return. That evening she mumbled something to her parents and the following morning the hospital staff were jubilant. Maria was speaking. The light had appeared at the end of the tunnel.

Hard work lay ahead but now there was a note of joy and more assurance in the air. Maria had to learn everything from scratch; how to eat, how to read and write. It was like teaching a baby. Her healing is an ongoing process and the psychologist says there is no limit to the extent of her recovery.

Recently Maria and her parents were with our

group in London at one of our healing services. They all looked so happy and well. The healing process involved everyone; a joint undertaking with everyone using their skills. It was a healing which had the added dimension of faith, hope and love.

Maria's story has a message for us all. Love and sharing can work wonders when we have faith. We continue to pray for Maria and for her ongoing healing and for all those who like her need our loving, prayerful support. Not long ago she wrote to me. Her mother told me her right hand, like her writing, is perfectly normal. Isn't that a wonderful story?

Father, your Son Jesus Christ promised that where two or three are gathered in his name great healings would be performed; we thank you for the love of the Holy Spirit poured forth on our Christian community, so that together we share in love the healing power of Christ, and remain open to each other and to you who want to heal us in our relationships with you, with each other and within ourselves.

9

Simplicity

Let the little children come to me for it is to such as these that the kingdom of heaven belongs.
(Matthew 19:14)

I want to tell you about a great friend of mine. I met her for the first time over twenty years ago. She was travelling round England speaking about the poor for whom she cared. She was unashamedly begging on their behalf. She had no hall available to her in Leeds so I offered her the use of my chapel.

When I met her, I knew at once that here was someone very special. The eyes which shone out of her weather-beaten face spoke of deep compassion and love. She was so pathetic, so small – five foot nothing – that one warmed to her. Here was a pilgrim Christian. In the chapel when she spoke to her audience of her love for the poor they were spellbound. The poor were her special concern. You could have heard a pin drop. She captured their hearts and there was hardly a dry eye in the place.

Today she is world famous; winner of the Nobel Peace Prize, showered with honours by countries, entertained by kings, popes and heads of state. The world is her oyster, and yet she has not changed one bit. She is still as humble as the day I first met her. I am talking, of course, about Mother Teresa of Calcutta.

At the end of her talk in our chapel, Mother Teresa spoke individually to each person, young and old. She looked so tiny and frail with many people towering above her, and yet one knew that in that small physical frame there was something special that reached out to everyone, rich or poor. It was her love which was gentle and caring. Now I had been trying for years without success to encourage a friend of mine in the audience to return to the practice of his Christian faith. He was a very sophisticated, down-to-earth person who wanted a reason for everything; yet a personal greeting from her on her tour of the chapel changed his life. 'What did she say?' I asked. He replied, 'God love and bless you!' 'But,' I said, 'I have been saying that to you for years and it didn't seem to work.' 'Ah,' he replied, 'but she said it by the way she lived – through her life – and I realized that God was so real to her that he came alive for me.'

What is so special about Mother Teresa? The answer is her humility, her gentleness, her caring for people. She has captivated the world because she has captured people's hearts.

The world today needs more Mother Teresas. People want to feel God's love come alive for them in their world. They long to reach out and touch someone who is good and gentle because

11

in some way this person reflects for them God's love. When such a person says to you, 'God love and bless you', then your life is changed in a way which you cannot explain. But you know you have met someone very, very special who will always remain your friend.

Father, your message of love for everyone is best spoken by those whose simple way of life gives a depth to their words which makes others aware of your abiding care and concern; teach us today and always to be simple, loving and honest in all our dealings with those with whom we share life's pilgrimage.

Money

You cannot be the slave both of God and of money. (Luke 16:13)

Do you find some of the sayings of Jesus disturbing? I do. Take for instance the time when he said to the rich young man, 'Sell what you own, give the money to the poor, then come follow me.'

Is it really necessary to be so drastic about our worldly possessions if we want to be Christians? Isn't Jesus being a bit over-dramatic with the rich man? Perhaps! But I have a sneaking feeling that somewhere along the line we have got a little bit greedy about money. We think that it can buy everything including happiness. Yet if money becomes our God it can destroy us.

Let me give you an example. Frank has been a friend of mine for many years. When I knew him first he was struggling financially, but from the outset I could see how ambitious he was. He had a restlessness within him to succeed which was, I suppose, a compensation for the fact that his parents were poor. He was happily married, with a loving wife and a young daughter. He started a little business on his own, and spent more and

13

more hours away from home as his business expanded.

He spent little time with his family, even though he surrounded them with all the trappings of wealth. The end of the story is sad. His wife divorced him, and is now living happily in a simple, uncomplicated way. His daughter's life is in a mess. She has rejected her father, and his way of life completely. The last time I heard of her she was in trouble with the police over drugs.

And Frank? He is still going from strength to strength, but inner peace is something he has not known for years. There are times when he has been the worse for drink, when he complains bitterly about his 'ungrateful' wife and daughter. He destroyed himself and his family because of his obsession with money. He forgot to give them his time and love.

There are hundreds of Franks in our world; people who want to be considered successful in the world's eyes, but who miss out on the really important things in life. I know that if I live for myself alone, then eventually I shall have only myself to live with. Fear of losing out, of not keeping up materially with others, is just plain stupid. Jesus tells the rich man that if we really want to be his followers then we must be prepared to share what we have with others less fortunate than ourselves.

Why? Because we are only pilgrims in this village we call the Earth. What you and I have been given is to be used – not only money but talents as well. None of us walks alone in this world.

Jesus' gospel, therefore, is telling us not to get a 'thing' about wealth, but to concentrate on loving and serving God, and sharing with our neighbour. Of course there are times when our sharing is abused and we tend to draw back in on ourselves. But in the end life is all about sharing with those round us; helping people in all sorts of ways. And in the sharing we are the ones who really receive because deep inside us we know that we are only doing what Jesus would do if he were in our situation. This is the source of our real peace and happiness.

Father, may we rest our lives in you who knows and provides for all our needs; give us a correct attitude to the material goods of this world so that we may never get our relationship with those we love out of focus, or endanger our deep inner peace, and awareness that you love us as we are, and not for what we achieve by worldly standards.

The Church is People

*Among the pagans the rulers lord it over them,
and the great men make their authority felt. This
is not to happen among you!* (Matthew 20:26)

Jesus was a revolutionary where religion was concerned. For him the Sabbath was made for man
and not man for the Sabbath. In his life he put
people first. There was a time in my ministry when
I needed to be reminded of this. And the unlikely
person who did it was Mary. Let me tell you the
story.

Mary was a blunt Yorkshire lass. Whatever else
about her, you knew where you stood with her.
She lived alone in a council flat in a working-class
part of Leeds. She came to Mass at St Patrick's
every morning hail, rain or snow. St Pat's was the
centre of her life. Every Monday and Friday she
spent the whole day sweeping, scrubbing and pol-
ishing the church. It was a very special place for
her with memories going back to her childhood
days.

In the 1960's I had just returned from teaching
in Rome and was sent to St Patrick's to liven
things up. The parish was becoming run down and

16

the people were very traditional. Change was in the air especially in the Church. I wanted our parish to be with it. I loved the people. They were the salt of the earth, and I prayed they would soon follow the lead I was giving.

One Monday morning I met Mary in church, on her knees as usual, scrubbing the floor. 'Mary,' I said, 'do you like what I am doing here? Do you agree with all the changes?' She paused, looked me straight in the eyes and said with great feeling: 'I don't like it one little bit. Why don't you leave the church as it is. It was all right before you came. And it'll be all right when you've gone.' I lost my cool for a few seconds. 'I didn't ask to come here,' I said. 'No,' she replied as quick as a whippet, 'and we didn't ask to have you.'

I retired from the scene of battle leaving Mary with the scrubbing and me licking my wounds. But Mary was right. It was her church before I came, and it would be hers when I moved on to pastures new. After all, the Church is about people. We have to love them, to take them as we find them. It is not about ideas or change or 'being with it'.

Next Sunday morning at Mass, I knew my sermon had changed in its approach because I had changed. I caught Mary's eye but her face showed no sign of response. I went into the church the following morning and there she was scrubbing away as usual. We spoke for a few minutes and as I was leaving her to go back into the house she said: 'Father, your sermon wasn't so bad yesterday. I think you might learn a few things if you stay long enough.'

Mary and I became great friends during my stay at St Pat's. When she died some years later, I buried her and we sang all the old hymns she loved so well. Yes, I hope I did learn a few things at St Pat's, like liking and loving people as they are and allowing God to change them in his time and not in ours. Mary was blunt but she was special. St Pat's meant a lot to her because it was for her God's home. She taught me that people come first before anything else. They did for Jesus. They did for Mary. And I hope they do for you and me.

Father, you sent your Son Jesus Christ as the servant of all and having compassion on the people he took them where he found them and as a kindly shepherd he showed them the way to you; teach us always to see ourselves as part of a loving, caring, sharing community in which we learn from each other the gentle service and mastery of Christ.

Peacemakers

Happy the peacemakers: they shall be called sons of God. (Matthew 5:9)

Northern Ireland is a divided land; Belfast a divided city. Protestants and Catholics are separated by a huge wall ironically called the Peace Line. Yet today in a city which has seen so much tragedy, hope is in the air again for some young people, through the vision and openness of one man. He is Father Myles Kavanagh. Let me tell you about him.

Father Myles was for many years parish priest of the Ardoyne, one of the most deprived and violent areas of Belfast. Eighty per cent of his young Catholic people were unemployed and relatively easy prey for recruitment to the IRA. On the border between his parish and a very tough Protestant ghetto, the other side of the Peace Line, was a disused factory. The windows were bricked up, and the walls, covered with massive graffiti, showed the hopelessness of the situation. Father Myles saw the factory, however, as a challenge to the city and its people, but above all to himself. His idea was to encourage young men

19

and women on the dole, as well as young university graduates, to start up their own businesses. The parish priest of the Ardoyne became managing director of the factory. Today over five hundred young people from both sides of the Peace Line work side by side in the same building. As one Protestant lad said to me, 'If we work together and for each other, then it is hardly likely we're going to fight each other.'

These young people under Father Myles' leadership have started Community Aid Projects for all the old people of the area. They decorate houses, repair furniture, radios and television sets. A young girl summed up their fresh attitude to the community. 'There is no such thing,' she said, 'as a Catholic television set to be repaired for Catholic old people. There are just old people who want their sets repairing and we want to do it.'

But it is not all sunshine. Some diehards say they have seen it all before in Belfast – how peace efforts blossom and soon die. Father Myles is quite realistic about the situation. 'We have had our ups and downs,' he said. 'Our factory may not be the answer to Belfast's problem, but we have to do our best to keep the candle of hope burning brightly.'

Today there are no graffiti on the factory walls. The factory itself is almost totally renovated, and the complex completely let. Some years ago, the young people who worked there slipped rather furtively into the factory. Today they have no such attitudes or fears.

Father Myles and the young people of West Belfast have a message for us. In our lives perhaps we have built a wall between ourselves and others. The bricks we use are prejudice, distrust, lack of forgiveness, social status, jealousy and a thousand and one other divisive things. If we use instead, bricks of love, understanding, caring and sharing, then perhaps we could build a bridge which unites rather than a wall which divides. St Paul said Christ was the peace between us because he had broken down the barrier which used to keep us apart. So don't build walls. Be like Father Myles and his young people. Build bridges instead.

Father, peace is the great gift of your Son to our world; help us to be peacemakers in all we say and do, so that we may build bridges which bring people together and not walls which divide and segregate them. In areas of violence and distrust may we, by our loving understanding, always be part of the solution, never part of the problem.

Influences

I am the vine, you are the branches. Whoever remains in me, with me in him, bears fruit in plenty. (John 15:5)

We all have good days and bad days. Some days may start off well but become utter chaos, as we don't seem to be able to get a thing right. And then at the end of the day something happens which makes it all worth while. I had such a day a few months ago.

I came to London for two very important interviews. I was in top form when I left York. Then everything started to go wrong. My train broke down just outside Peterborough and was ninety minutes late arriving at King's Cross. Too late for my first meeting. My frustration was beginning to show because that was the big one as far as I was concerned, and the reason I came to London.

I went to the second meeting but quite honestly it was a waste of time. My spirits were pretty low because I was thinking of all I could be doing if I had stayed at home. I decided to cut my losses and get an earlier train back to York. I was walking along Oxford Street to the nearest tube station when the rain came down. I left home in brilliant sunshine so I had no raincoat or umbrella. I sheltered for some time under a shop front but the rain showed no sign of relenting. I felt like Noah in the Ark letting out the doves to see if the floods had subsided.

I lost my patience and ran down the street getting more drenched every minute, when I heard a voice calling my name 'Michael Buckley', 'Michael Buckley'. I looked behind me and there was a tall, bearded young man running after me: quite an awesome sight. I stopped in my tracks. What on earth was this all about? Did he want a little help from a rain-soaked clergyman? Some warm soup on a bad day? I'd had a bad day myself, so being a martyr I listened! He was all excited. 'Don't you remember me? I came to the courses at your centre. I was there the night Mother Teresa of Calcutta came. You spoke to us after she had gone, and you said that there was greatness in all of us. I never forgot that. It went round and round in my mind. It changed my life so much that now I'm a doctor looking after lepers in India. It is all thanks to you and what you said.'

Then I remembered him. The carefree young university student with the mischievous eyes. 'Tom, I remember you well.' 'Wasn't it great that we met here today?' he said. 'I'm sure God meant it to happen because I wanted to say thank you for all you did for me.' 'I did nothing', I said, as I gave him the warmest hug ever seen between two men in pouring rain in Oxford Street. Soon he was gone to catch his train home, and I to catch mine.

Suddenly it was no longer raining. My suit was dripping wet but my heart was full of joy. What a wonderful day in London, and fancy meeting Tom again! On the train I thought how much we influence each other for good without ever realizing it. Much that is of value in our lives has come about through someone saying something that helps to change our lives. The sayings of Jesus Christ have done that for me.

Back at York, train on time. Good day? Yes. The meetings? I think I made the most important one.

Father, you know that every word we speak, or action we do, has its influence on those whom we meet in our daily lives; may all we say and do this day be under the influence of the Holy Spirit, so that people may know your power and presence in their lives.

Pets and Happiness

Look at the birds in the sky, they do not sow or reap or gather into barns, yet your heavenly Father feeds them. (Matthew 6:26)

There are times when tragedy hits us so hard that we think we will never rise again. Yet when days are dark, if we remain *open* to things round us, God will lift the gloom in the most unexpected way. This happened to Bob and Wendy, two very dear friends of mine.

They have recently celebrated their wedding anniversary, and they are very happy and fulfilled now, but I knew them both when they were lonely and felt that life had come to an end. They both lost their partners in the most tragic circumstances.

For over eighteen years Wendy was happily married to Robert, and they had three lovely children. While they were on holiday in Spain Robert died suddenly of a heart attack. The weeks and months that followed were, for Wendy, full of shadow and despair. Her consolation lay in her children. Her pet dog also seemed to sense, as animals often do, what she was going through.

At the same time Bob, who lived nearby, was suffering a similar dark experience. He had just lost his wife Mary, who died after a long harrowing illness. Bob could not imagine life without her. Even though he had a thriving business and two very loving children, life for him had lost its meaning. He withdrew more and more within himself until he was in danger of becoming a recluse. He rarely went out except to exercise his dog.

Late one autumn afternoon as he was walking down a country lane near his home he noticed a lady with a dog coming towards him. Soon the two dogs began to play together. Their antics among the fallen leaves took Bob out of himself. For the first time in months he laughed. So did Wendy, the owner of the other dog. In their grief they had remained open to their dogs, and God used this openness to bring them together. They began to talk to each other, and in their conversation discovered a whole new world outside themselves. It was as though they had known each other all their lives. 'We knew at that moment,' said Wendy, 'that God meant us for each other. We walked towards each other on that leafy lane as if God had planned it from all time. Our pain and loneliness had prepared us for each other. We knew God meant us to live a new life and to be happy together.'

They invited me to officiate at their wedding service, and I wanted it to be very special and to unite both families in a new bond. The children wrote all the prayers and planned the service.

Wendy's son gave her away and Bob's son was his best man.

Today both families live very happily in the same house. The two dogs still run round the place. You could say they brought Bob and Wendy together, and I believe it was all part of God's plan. It was not by accident that they met that autumn afternoon. God had always been watching over them even in their loneliness. So the one thing in life we need to remember is that we are never alone, especially when days are dark. God is with us always. 'Though I should walk in the valley of death no evil will I fear. You are there with your crook and your staff. With these you give me comfort.'

God, loving creator of all life, help us to treat with compassion the living creatures entrusted to our care; may we respond to their loyalty to us by showing them that in a special way under your gentle guidance they are for our happiness and fulfilment in your loving creation.

The Goodness Within

Jesus looked up and spoke to him: 'Zaccheus, come down. Hurry, because I must stay at your house today.' (Luke 19:5)

We think we know people. But we don't really. Why? Because we like to slot them into convenient pigeon-holes, to put a tag on them so that when we look at the tag we think we know the person. It's treating people like mass-produced, off-the-peg clothes. And yet people are individuals. But we never seem to give them a chance to be themselves. Jesus did. The Bible is full of stories of how he saw and assessed people as they were in themselves. Jesus scandalized many people of his time because he refused to take on board their judgement of others. He made his own mind up, no matter what the profession was of the person concerned. He stood respectability on its head because sometimes he chose to number people of very doubtful backgrounds and professions among his friends.

My favourite story is about Zaccheus. He wanted to see Jesus, and because he was so small he had to climb a sycamore tree to get a glimpse of him as he passed by in the crowd underneath. Jesus stopped, called him down, and said he wanted to spend the rest of the day in his company, in his house. The crowd was furious. Didn't he know that Zaccheus was a senior tax collector and had made a fortune out of his profession? 'They all complained when they saw what was happening', wrote St Luke; 'He has gone to stay at a sinner's house', they said. But their judgement of Zaccheus was completely wrong. Zaccheus in fact could say, and said, to Jesus, 'Sir, if I have cheated anybody I will pay him back four times the amount. I am going to give half my property to the poor.' Which one of his detractors could match that?

Well I have met many Zaccheuses in my life. People whose professional image in our pigeon-hole way of looking at them did not do justice to the kind of person they really were in themselves. Alec is one of them. He is a policeman who retired recently after over thirty years service. He is my friend, and I know that what he says of himself is true. 'Never once in my life have I used violence against anyone. My truncheon was an ornament on my belt. And, mind you, I have been in some tough situations. But the most I ever did was to speak firmly, and let the bullies know I meant business. And it worked. Today we live in a world full of violence. When I see all the fighting and hassle I feel sick deep inside me. It seems all wrong. I have never lied to gain a conviction, and I wouldn't be put off giving evidence if I thought someone was guilty. I am proud of the little I have done to keep our country safe for ordinary people to live in peace. And I don't consider myself a great fellow. Just an ordinary bloke doing an ordinary job.'

Now Alec doesn't go to church and he doesn't look on himself as a very religious man. And yet he has got his standards and values right. His lifestyle has a lot to say to all of us. I'm not saying that all policemen are like Alec, or all tax collectors like Zaccheus, but some are. Maybe more than we think. It is not what people look like on the outside that matters but what they do with their lives.

So perhaps we might take a closer look at people as Jesus did. Then perhaps we will be surprised and gladdened at the goodness we will find. We say we want to live in peace and are prepared to work for it. In our lives I hope we can identify with Alec and thousands like him who in their ordinary way and in the jobs they do day in day out help to create an atmosphere of peace. Together with them we can be peace-makers for our world.

Father, your Son Jesus Christ when he was on earth enjoyed the company of publicans and sinners because he knew the good that was within people. Teach us to live with everyone with such love and peace as Jesus did, that we may never prejudge people harshly or speak the cruel word, but always seek to encourage what is good in others so that our society may be blessed with harmony, goodwill and peace.

The Child Within

Jesus took a little child, set him in front of them, put his arms around him and said: 'Anyone who welcomes one of these little children in my name welcomes me.' (Mark 9:36–37)

There is a child in all of us. If we want to be happy, really happy, then the child in us must remain part of us. This way of thinking is very much in line with the teaching of Jesus. Time and again he stressed that unless we become as little children we will miss out on life and not really understand his message.

He said his gospel was for those whose approach to life remained simple and uncomplicated because at heart they were children. And being children has nothing to do with age. You can be five or sixty-five and still be a child at heart. It is all a question of attitude. Countless times I have seen how young and old are one in mind and heart. For them there is no age barrier when they are sharing their experiences.

Recently on Scarborough beach I was watching an elderly man playing with his grandson in the sand. The little blond child was aged about four.

31

The man taught him how to make sand-castles and then build a wall against the incoming tide. They worked together as partners. The years slipped away and I was young again, building my sand-castles on a far-off beach in Ireland. The old man and his grandson had unknowingly invited me to share with them in their joy and happiness because it was also part of my life and memory as a child.

A few days later, quite by chance, I met the old man in a supermarket shopping with his wife. I told him how fascinated I was by what I had seen on the beach, and what it did for me. The old man's face came alive in one huge smile. 'That little boy, John,' he said, 'is my youngest grandchild. I have played on the beach with all my grandchildren and I have enjoyed them all, every one of them. They have all been different and they have all kept me young. They bring me back to the days when I was a wee lad, and I used to come on holidays with my parents to Scarborough. So I am a child again here when I play with John. I think I get even more happiness from it now. I don't know why, but I do. I suppose it is because it is so simple and carefree, and such a contrast to the hustle and bustle of everyday living.'

The young boy and his grandfather were happy in each other's company. What they built was of no material consequence; the sea soon wiped away all trace of their sand-castles. But what they shared together was priceless. They had made a memory. They shared peace and joy which are gifts for the simple, the young at heart. To look at the stars at night or identify with the different moods of the sea, or to envy a bird as it floats effortlessly through the air. These are for our peace and happiness. A perpetual source of wonder. But sometimes we become so trapped and weighed down with the cares of life that we miss out on the simple things. That is why we need to keep alive the child within us. To build castles in the sand. To be for ever young. This is the recipe Jesus gives us for happiness. And the young at heart know what he means.

Father, we are for ever children at heart and in the simple things of life we find our deepest contentment: may we always share with the young who by what they say and do remind us of our own youth. Help us never to outgrow the present world in which we live, and may the Indian summer of our days be shot through with the brightness of your presence which was with us even when you formed us in our mother's womb.

Travelling Light

Jesus instructed them to take nothing for the journey except a staff – no bread, no haversack, no coppers for their purses. (Mark 6:8)

Some sayings of Jesus seem impossible to follow. Take, for instance, his instruction to his seventy-two followers when he sent them out on their first mission. They were to take nothing for the journey, no bread, no haversack, no coppers for their purses. They were to wear sandals but he added, 'Do not take a spare tunic' (Mark 6:8–9). It's what we call 'travelling light'! Do you know of anyone who travels light like that? I do. Just one. And she travels the world. Her name? Mother Teresa of Calcutta.

Let me tell you an amusing story about the embarrassment she caused on one occasion because she travelled light. I had arranged for her to speak some years ago at our conference centre in Wetherby, Yorkshire. It was one of her first visits to this country from India and because her schedule was tight it was arranged that she would fly from London to our regional airport. I informed the airport manager and he immediately set the VIP process into operation. 'She is an international figure,' he said, 'and we're going to do her proud. We'll pull out all the stops for her.' And he certainly did.

Everybody who was anybody locally looked resplendent in their chains of office and special hats that would make the ladies of Ascot decidedly envious. Yes, it was an impressive galaxy to meet Mother as she stepped off the plane clutching her little plastic carrier-bag.

There were introductions and handshakes all round, and the usual kind of chatter which makes sound without conversation. After twenty or so minutes of this, I noticed out of the corner of my eye an airport official whispering something into the manager's ear. Quickly the manager came to me very upset and said, 'We can't find Mother Teresa's luggage anywhere. It's not on the plane. We've checked with London and they have no trace of it there. What are we going to do?' I calmed him down. I had met Mother before, and knew her style of life. I went over to Mother and asked her where was her luggage. 'Here,' she replied, holding up her little plastic carrier-bag. 'But your things you brought on your journey from India. Where are they?' I asked. 'They're here,' she replied with a smile, 'it's all I need.' All Mother was carrying were the barest toilet requisites and a spare sari. The sigh of the manager when I told him was one of relief tinged with amazement.

So Jesus' advice, and Mother Teresa's motto, is 'travel light'. So many of us, not only on our

35

holidays, but in our everyday lives, carry far too much luggage. We surround ourselves with things we don't need because we can't let go of possessions. We never know the freedom of travelling light. The important things to carry are within ourselves. Inner peace and love for those we meet on our travels through life.

Mother Teresa, however, didn't quite keep to the gospel instructions of Jesus. True, she was barefoot and wore the cheapest of sandals. But she did carry a spare sari. I think the Good Lord would allow her that little extra going through His Customs.

Father, provider of all our needs, grant that we always remain simple and unaffected by power and wealth in our journey through life, and remain secure in the knowledge that the only thing we really need to carry into our eternal home is your love, which we pray will shine through us today on all whom we meet, and with whom we share our pilgrimage.

Storm on a Lake

He rebuked the wind and said to the sea, 'Quiet now! Be calm!' And the wind dropped and all was calm again. (Mark 4:39)

I don't like storms.

There have been times at sea when I thought our boat would never make land. A plane in which I was travelling some years ago had one of its engines knocked out by lightning and had to make a forced landing. All rather hair-raising stuff. But I never experienced a storm on a lake . . . that is, until recently. I didn't believe it could be so frightening. Let me tell you about it.

I was on my holidays in Switzerland and on a late sunny afternoon I went on a boat trip round the top of Lake Geneva. Everyone was enjoying the beautiful weather with the sunshine pouring out of a clear blue sky. An ideal way to spend a summer afternoon. As we passed Montreux, we saw a man fishing from his little boat, a perfect picture of contentment. Most of the passengers waved to him and he waved back. We seemed to sense that we were enjoying ourselves without a care in the world. We were all relaxed and happy.

An hour later on our return journey the scene had changed completely. A black cloud appeared from nowhere and suddenly there was a torrential rain sweeping across our boat. This was soon followed by ear-splitting peals of thunder and flashes of fork lightning. The waves stirred up by the gale-force winds lashed against the side of our boat and we were tossed about like a cork in the water. It chilled the heart and the contrast in such a short space of time left me confused and shaken.

All round us was black as night. Suddenly two rescue speedboats with lights flashing came out of the gloom and headed in the direction where we had waved to our fisherman friend a short while before. I prayed and hoped he was all right. Actually he was rescued. The storm lasted thirty minutes until finally we limped to the jetty and ran for shelter from the lashing rain.

That night as I lay in bed I realized even more dramatically how dangerous the situation was, and how lucky we were to be alive and how quickly and easily the peace of the afternoon was disturbed. And peace is very easily disturbed. When we think that everything is plainsailing in our lives along comes some unexpected storm and we are thrown off balance. Someone dear to us dies, our job and lifestyle are threatened, or everything round us seems to be falling apart. That is the time when we need faith that all will be well, God is looking after us, the storm will soon pass.

For the first time in my life, only now am I beginning to understand the Bible story of the calming of the storm by Jesus on Lake Galilee. It was just like my own experience.

'It began to blow a gale,' writes Mark, 'and the waves were breaking into the boat so that it was almost swamped. But Jesus was in the stern, his head on the cushion asleep. They woke him and said to him, "Master, do you not care? We are going down!" And he woke up and rebuked the wind and said to the sea, "Quiet now! Be calm!" And the wind dropped, and all was calm again. Then he said to them, "Why are you so frightened? How is it that you have no faith?" '

We all need faith amid the storms of life that in these storms Jesus is with us. He may be asleep but he is still there. And he won't mind if we wake him and ask him to help us. He will calm the storm and bring us peace.

Father, you watch over us every moment of our lives; be with us this day so that when we are tempted through unsuspected happenings to lose our serenity of mind and peace of heart, then may your Son Jesus rebuke the inner storms which threaten us, and by the power of your Spirit, may we be calm again knowing that you are always near, if only we have the faith to believe in your abiding and never-failing love and protection.

Living One Day at a Time

> *Do not say, 'What are we to eat? What are we to drink?' Your heavenly Father knows you need them all.* (Matthew 6:31–32)

Have you a favourite passage in the New Testament? I suppose we all have. May I share one of mine with you? It is from Matthew's Gospel, chapter 6, verses 25–34: 'That is why I am telling you not to worry about your life and what you are to eat, nor about your body and how you are to clothe it. Surely life means more than food and the body more than clothing! . . . So do not worry; do not say, "What are we to eat? What are we to drink? How are we to be clothed?" It is the pagans who set their hearts on all these things. Your heavenly Father knows you need them all . . . So do not worry about tomorrow: tomorrow will take care of itself. Each day has enough trouble of its own.'

A worried person for Jesus is a divided person – not at peace – whatever the cause of his worry, because through worry he cannot live the present moment to the full.

Once I trust God with my life, I shall soon

discover that he has a delicious sense of humour. What his Son did in Cana of Galilee, to save the young couple faced with the problem of a lack of wine for their guests, he does for us each day, if only we knew it.

Here is an example from my own life. When the Wood Hall Centre at Wetherby in Yorkshire was first opened we were not as organized on the staff as we might have been. One Sunday afternoon three coach loads of old people turned up to look around the place. We were tired after a heavy weekend conference, and were shattered when the trip organizers told us that they had ordered high tea. We had no record of such a request on our files, and there was literally nothing in the larder. Sister Jarlath, our cook, threw her hands up in despair, and said to me: 'This is too much. I suppose you expect God to come down and get a high tea for a hundred and fifty people.' I laughed, but it was rather hollow, as I shepherded our visitors to the chapel for an unscheduled Mass, where, tongue in cheek, I asked them to pray for a minor miracle. Ironically, the Gospel reading for the Sunday was the feeding of the five thousand in the desert, which I thought was rubbing liturgical salt in an open wound.

When we came back to the centre, there before my astonished eyes was a magnificent meal of cooked hams, cakes of every variety, jellies and fruit. I had previously thought the cook was superb, but this was miraculous! 'Where did you get all the food from in such record time?' I asked her, 'with all the shops shut?' She told me the story. Just *after* I had started Mass, the Little Sisters of the Poor came in their van with the leftovers from their garden fête held the previous day. They thought we might be able to make use of the food and they did not want to see it going to waste. How right they were! 'Who told you we needed it?' I asked them. They replied, 'No one. We just thought we would bring it.' These Little Sisters do wonderful work looking after old people, and it was to old people that the meal was in fact given. The bewildered Sister Jarlath, with a twinkle in her eye, said: 'I have seen everything now. I will never doubt again!' Who said God has not got a sense of humour? God runs the best catering service in the world, because his shop is open twenty-four hours a day, seven days a week, and his only price is trust in his providence.

Each day has its own problems. These problems become worries when I keep them over from yesterday, or even anticipate tomorrow's. God gives us life one day at a time. He walks with me in my life today, if I trust him with all my yesterdays, and tomorrows. My constant prayer every morning is, 'One day at a time, Lord Jesus, one day at a time.'

Why don't you try it. It really does work.

Father, teach us to rest in your loving care, so as not to worry about what tomorrow may bring, and may we be secure in the knowledge that you will provide for all our needs, because you are a loving

42

Father who has the power and the will to help us, and you know our needs even before the words of petition are on our lips.

Conversion

May they all be one. Father, may they be one in us, as you are in me and I am in you, so that the world may believe it was you who sent me. (John 17:21)

In 1988 we celebrated the 250th anniversary of the conversion of John Wesley. His life was changed on the 24th May 1738 when he met a group of Christians who really believed in Jesus as a personal Saviour. It clicked with Wesley, and as he wrote himself, 'my heart was warmed with what I experienced', and from that simple happening a whole movement of deep Christian spirituality was born.

Margaret had a similar experience to John Wesley. Here is how she told me the story of her conversion. 'For years,' she wrote to me, 'I was a deeply committed member of my church. I believed not so much in a personal God who was the Father of all Christians, but in a God who was the exclusive property of our church. He was our God and nobody else's. I became so involved with the little things of our group, the nuts and bolts of our church, that I began to think because we were doing so well that we could get on without him. He was there when we needed him, but it was more important to be accepted and loved in our fellowship than it was to know God as a Father who loved us personally. Oh yes, many was the time I proclaimed Jesus as my personal Saviour, and God the Father as someone whose personal love for me was indispensable, but they were words which through repetition no longer penetrated my mind and heart. They were words without any real effect on my life. And suddenly I became aware that I needed healing in order to renew my Christian faith. It was shattering for me to discover how shallow it had become.

'I came with some friends to a healing service at which you and your team ministered. There I discovered, as if for the first time and in a truly caring atmosphere, what my Christian faith was all about, and what it meant to me. I knew then that God had no favourites, and that he wanted me to share my new-found faith with everyone. I am still a member of my church, but in a new way. I know now that it is a loving, caring community which makes us aware of Jesus as our personal Saviour.'

Today Margaret works with our healing team. She is a bridge-builder because of her own conversion experience, and she knows that faith without love is meaningless. From my own experience I know that people today will only believe in a loving God if they can see him at work in our lives. They don't want us to talk about him; they want to touch him in us. This is what John Wesley,

Margaret and thousands like them saw as the essence of the Christian gospel.

Today, as we give thanks for John Wesley's openness to the Spirit, perhaps we might listen again to God's voice when he tells us that he loves us as a Father. He speaks to us in simple ways. But we must be prepared to change. To be converted. And then life will take on a new meaning.

Father, we praise and thank you for our Christian faith which is your gift to us. Bless all Christians of all denominations who pray, work and strive for unity so that they may continue their work of bridge-building. We are all enriched by each other's gifts and ministries, and the source of these is the Holy Spirit who transforms our set attitudes of religion into a living faith whose witness the world needs if it is to believe in the power and resurrection of your Son Jesus Christ.

The Prodigal Father

*The father said, 'We are going to have a feast,
a celebration, because this son of mine was dead
and has come back to life; he was lost and is
found.' And they began to celebrate.* (Luke
15:24)

Time and again in my life I come across people
who bring the gospel of Jesus Christ alive for me.
For example, I thought I knew what the story of
the Prodigal Son was all about until I met Jane
and her father, Philip. Since I met them the story
of the rich son who squandered his money and
came home penniless to a loving, forgiving father
has taken on a new meaning. Let me tell you
about Jane and her father.

Philip is a typically happy person who loves life,
his wife and his children, who are now all grown
up and living away from home. Through the years
no matter what happened his children all knew
their father loved them. He didn't spoil them. But
his love was something they could count on when
the dice seemed loaded against them.

If he had a favourite it was Jane. She was his
eldest daughter, and to this day she retains a dis-

arming simplicity which touches a deep chord in her father's heart. After an excellent convent and university education, against all the odds she joined the hippie movement. This really hurt Philip and went against the grain of his thoroughly Catholic British upbringing. But sadly he let her go. Whenever she got in contact with home that was a day of rejoicing but these occasions were less frequent than her father would have desired.

One day when I was visiting her parents she appeared on the scene. She was badly dressed and looked grossly undernourished. Her parents nursed her back to health again. They prayed, as did I, that she would stay with them and settle down. But it was not to be. Soon she was on the road again and for the umpteenth time Philip stood at the door to wave her goodbye.

Recently she settled down with a partner to a very bohemian style of life far away from home. She is a mother of a baby girl of whom Philip is justifiably proud. He still hopes she will return home but while there is sadness deep within him there is no anger or bitterness. 'She is my daughter,' he says, 'I love her. I always will. Of course I wanted a different lifestyle for her. But she chose to live this way and I can't stop being her father just because of that. My home is hers whenever or if ever she wants to come. I want her happiness but I still hope that things will change.'

So now, through my dear friend Philip, I get a glimpse of what God's love for us as a father must be really like. He never stops loving us even when we wander far away from him in our style of life.

In the Bible story it isn't the son who is prodigal with his money. It is the father who is prodigal with his love. Jane is lucky to have Philip as her father. But he reckons that he is the fortunate one. 'Jane,' he says, 'is my blessing, my daughter.'

Father, you have no favourites because you love us all in a personal, unique way. I thank you that you have always welcomed me in loving forgiveness despite the many times I have strayed from you. Teach me that in all situations you are there wanting me home and preparing a celebration for me. May this saving thought keep me close to you always, never to leave you again because I have known you and called you Father.

Christ the Shepherd

I am the good shepherd: the good shepherd is one who lays down his life for his sheep. (John 10:11)

We don't understand many of the images in the gospel, mainly because we live in a different age. Christ, for example, saw his role as that of a shepherd. Because most of us live in cities we have little experience of what a shepherd is except what we imagine him to be from television's *One Man and his Dog*. But I really got an insight into what Christ meant about being a shepherd when I lived in Italy as a student.

During the hot summer months we escaped to the hills outside Rome. Our college villa was situated overlooking a beautiful lake. Often I saw the shepherds taking their sheep down to graze on its steep sides. They were roughly dressed but they always carried a kind of bagpipes on their back. One night there was the most terrific electric storm which seemed to go on for hours. We were all pretty scared, especially when the lights in the villa failed. Through my open window, amid the peals of thunder, I could hear the most beautiful soothing music coming from somewhere beneath me on the lake's hillside. I listened enthralled. Soon my fear left me. I wondered who was the musician who could play such sensitive music. Surely a rough shepherd wouldn't produce music like that?

Next morning just after dawn I met the shepherd leading his sheep up from the lake. I asked him where the music came from. He tapped his bagpipes. 'My sheep get disturbed during a storm,' he said, 'so I bring this to play to them to keep them quiet.' I asked him to play for me and he shyly agreed. From his primitive instrument and rough hands came the haunting melody which the night before brought me peace. I closed my eyes in wonder at his sensitivity. So this simple man taught me to understand a little more of what Jesus meant by calling himself a shepherd. Someone who really cares for his flock, who stays with them through the storms of life and brings them peace.

We are all afraid at some periods of our life. We need to be soothed, reassured so that we can be at peace. Sometime today amid all the storms which may come our way perhaps we will hear the gentle music of the shepherd which brings us peace.

The music that we hear which brings us that peace are the words of Christ:

I am the good shepherd;
I know my own
and my own know me,

just as the Father knows me
and I know the Father;
and I lay down my life for my sheep.

*Father, there are many times when I am afraid
because there seems to be no direction in my life,
and I am not sure where I am going. It is at these
times when I seem lost and walking in the world
of shadows that I turn to your Son Jesus Christ,
the Good Shepherd who gave his life for his sheep,
knowing that he will lead me along the right path,
and keep me safe from harm. May I always hear
his voice amid the storms of life, and may it be
like music to my ears bringing me peace.*

Encouragement

Put your hope in God. He is your strength, so take heart. (Psalm 27:14)

We all need to be encouraged. To be praised. To be reassured that we are worthwhile people, and that our lives have a meaning. I want to encourage you not only to think well of yourself, but to lift others up and not knock them down. Encouragement is, after all, very much a Christian virtue.

Jesus was an encourager. He lifted people up when they were really down. He praised the most unlikely people, like tax collectors and women of the street. The only ones who felt the sharp edge of his tongue were the self-righteous pharisees, the holier-than-thou people who burdened everyone they met with unnecessary laws and insupportable guilt. He knew the damage they did to people's lives and so he gave them short shrift. Jesus was aware that all those round him, even his chosen disciples, needed encouragement, and so he devoted his life to doing just that. And those of us who follow in his way should encourage people to live as happy and meaningful a life as possible.

Jill's life was changed through encouragement. She had suffered grievously at the hands of her fiancé, a thoroughly selfish person, who so eroded her confidence that she felt no use to anyone, least of all to herself. When he walked out on her she attempted suicide. In order to avoid any more hurt she began to cut herself off from everyone. Previously she had been an excellent nurse, but soon her patients began to suffer because she was completely closed in on herself. A friend, one of the few who were left, brought her to us. We prayed and talked with her in a gentle way. Gradually she began to see that it was not the end of the world, that she had something to offer which people needed. She grappled with the feelings of rejection and acceptance within her, and eventually she dedicated herself with renewed energy and motivation to her nursing. We praised and encouraged her every step of the way.

Today she is a different person. Her life is all of a piece again. Her nursing is very much part of who she is. She is a great encourager of her patients because she has been through the valley of darkness herself. She met the right man in her life and is very happily married.

So today we remember Jesus' words of encouragement to his disciples, 'Courage, take heart. I love you and call you friend.' Perhaps if we feel useless we might take heart. Someone somewhere thinks we're great because he loves us. He makes our life worth living. So don't listen to those who knock us. Lift yourself up. Look around. So many people need a word of praise and reassurance. We can all help each other. So don't knock people, lift them up. You will be lifted up and encouraged too.

Father, you know what is in us, our weaknesses and our strengths. Teach us through your loving kindness and understanding to appreciate our real value in your eyes so that we may learn to use more and more creatively the gifts you have given to us; and in loving ourselves in a truly Christian way may we know, love and serve you better and as we have been encouraged by you may we do the same for those with whom we share our lives.

Life After Death

Blessed are those who mourn: they shall be comforted. (Matthew 5:5)

Christians are supposed to believe in life after death. Jesus promised eternal life to his followers. 'Anyone who believes in me,' he said, 'although he be dead he will live for ever.' And yet most Christians in my experience have a nagging suspicion that death is the end of everything. They mourn without hope because deep-down in their hearts they do not believe that they will ever see their loved ones again. We may think we believe in life after death until someone we love, and with whom we shared our lives, dies. Then the crunch comes. Do we really believe in the resurrection? It is at times like these that we have to measure our sense of loss against our faith.

Bridget had to do it and she came through but only after a long and lonely struggle. She was an excellent Christian whose husband died tragically in a car accident after twenty years of happily married life. For a long time afterwards she was 'lost' and no longer seemed to be 'alive'. Her peace of soul was profoundly disturbed. Her life, so full of joy before, now lay shattered in pieces round her. Apart from a faithful few, the many friends who were constant callers after his death rarely came to visit her. They had to get on with living their lives. So Bridget was forced to face the future more or less on her own.

She began to draw in on herself more and more so that her home became a prison, a museum, with memories of her husband. She was dead inside. Eventually she came to our group and together we prayed for her healing. There were some in our group who had experienced the same trauma of bereavement. Their words and presence helped her, and soon the tears flowed which washed away the sad ache in her heart. She spoke openly for the first time about her doubts and fears and set them against her faith. Her faith won. Today she truly believes that her husband is alive and shares in Christ's risen life, and that she will see him again. It is not something sentimental or wishful thinking, but something that is very much part of her life and happiness. My thoughts go out to all those who still walk in the valley of the shadow of bereavement. Take heart. Love never comes to an end. Imagine your dear one saying to you: 'Death is nothing, nothing at all. For I have only slipped away into the next room. Why should I be out of mind because I am out of sight? I am waiting for you somewhere near and all is well.'

Jesus through his resurrection promises life without end to all who believe in him. He is the resurrection for you, and me, and all those whom we love.

Father, look with pity on all those who walk in the vale of sorrow surrounded on all sides by the memory of their loved one whose loss has left a void in their lives. Give them a lively faith in the resurrection of your Son Jesus Christ so that the expectation of seeing their loved one again may give them strength to live the rest of their lives with sweet memories and joyful hope, so that the joy of the past with their loved one is but a foretaste of the happiness in the future which will never end.

Origins

Mary and Joseph went back to their own town of Nazareth. Meanwhile the child grew to maturity, and he was filled with wisdom; and God's favour was with him. (Luke 2:40)

I'm Irish and I'm very proud of it. Ireland and its culture will always remain very much part of me. In the summer of 1986 I went to visit my mother's birthplace. Even though it was the first time in over fifty years that I had returned, the people who had lived there for generations made me feel very much part of them as if I had never moved away at all. My mother's home had been modernized, but when I closed my eyes I could smell the turf and furze burning in the open hearth, and hear the music of the fiddle as we sang and danced our way through many a long evening in an Irish kitchen. The Irish certainly know how to enjoy themselves.

My grandparents were staunch patriots and only spoke Gaelic. I spent many a happy summer with them, and subconsciously I slipped into their native tongue and way of expressing things. How helpful it was in later life. Two years ago I was with a television crew in Northern Ireland, and after filming in the Bogside in Derry we went for a pub lunch. Unbeknown to us it was a nest for IRA sympathizers. I heard a group of them in a corner talking in Gaelic about us, and planning to set fire to our van and its valuable contents. I went over to them and upbraided them in their own language. Awe-struck, the would-be tough guys lapsed into silence. I hope my grandparents would have been proud of me, my Gaelic and my attitude. Sheepishly one by one they left the pub. Then we took over, and I led the rest of the bar in some rousing Irish choruses interlaced with some British songs which tempted Providence! The angels were watching over us, and soon afterwards we headed for Belfast with our film and dignity intact.

My roots are still very Irish, and the Irish are the butt of many jokes. My favourite Irish joke, which sums up my attitude, is of the Englishman who asked the Welshman, Scotsman and Irishman what they would like to be if they were not what they were. 'I'd be an Italian,' said the Welshman, 'because they have many fine operatic singers and choirs.' 'I'd be a Frenchman,' joined in the Scotsman, 'because they have an unending supply of beautiful wines.' The Irishman paused, obviously puzzled by the question. 'If I weren't Irish,' he said reflectively and slowly, 'God knows, I think I'd be ashamed.'

For all of my love of Ireland, I have chosen England as my home and Yorkshire is my favourite county. I regard Ireland as my mother and

England as my wife, and it grieves me to see any conflict between them. My prayer is for peace and harmony between all the peoples of these islands. We are one people with different cultures.

These different origins and cultures should teach us the ways of peace and tolerance, not divide us. Jesus never let people forget where he came from. His enemies could see nothing good coming from Nazareth, yet he himself was the true way of peace. When we appreciate the creative peaceful value of other cultures, then it will be a great day not only for the Irish but for the whole world.

Father, in whom alone are the roots of our being and fulfilment, I praise you for my roots which you planted in my native land. May I bring with me wherever I go what is best in my culture and tradition so that I may be a messenger of harmony, peace and the unity of all mankind.

Courage

Jesus called out to them, saying, 'Courage! It is I! Do not be afraid'. (Matthew 14:28)

This is a story about Alice. She is a very brave woman. All through her life she has had to face challenges that would have put a lesser person flat on her face. Not Alice. She is made of sterner stuff. She has a courage born of deep faith.

Thirty one years ago she married Joe, a land-scape gardener, and within six years they had two lovely, healthy daughters, Helen and Tina. They always wanted a son, and Joe was born in 1965. Their cup of joy was brimming over, but within eighteen months Joe was diagnosed as spastic. He could not go to an ordinary school, and never learned to read or write. But the love of his parents taught him other skills, and soon he was pottering round the garden with his Dad. Seven years ago the family moved to a new home with some adjoining land, and set up their own Garden Centre. Young Joe has such a natural skill for cultivating heather, conifers and shrubs that the business has grown, and now he is preparing his first illustrated book on gardening with the aid of a ghost-writer.

With few financial worries and young Joe doing so marvellously, their happiness was complete when Helen, their daughter, married seven years ago, and made Joe and Alice the proud grandparents of a bonny girl. But tragedy struck a cruel double blow four years later. Joe, Alice's husband, developed serious heart trouble, and Helen gave birth to twin daughters, one of whom, Carol, was a spina bifida. This meant that her backbone wasn't fully formed. The doctor said she would never walk, and of course this would affect her physical growth and mental outlook. But Alice never gave up. Her faith helped her to believe that better news was on the way as long as she could keep trusting in God.

So Alice brought the whole family over to one of our healing sessions in Yorkshire. She believed that God would help her husband, Joe, and her granddaughter, Carol, in a very special way. I have rarely met anyone with so much faith that everything would be well. She left the healing service all smiles and confidence, even though there was no physical change in either her husband or her granddaughter. But she knew that she herself had drawn courage from the service. And the answer? Four months ago out of the blue Carol was chosen by the Health Service from thousands of others for a mechanical tailor-made brace system. I saw her walking and laughing in young Joe's garden, the spina bifida girl enjoying the artistic work of her spastic uncle. And the father, Joe? Well, he had a successful heart operation and is still very much part of a happy family. Alice's faith and laughter never wavered or altered. 'I knew,' she said, 'God would help me when I asked him. I didn't know how, but he's never failed me before, and I knew when I left the chapel that day that he would look after Joe and Carol in his way. And he did.'

Father, in the midst of all our troubles you come to our aid. You do not help us before we have helped ourselves, but when we think we are at the end of our resources and cannot bear any more the burdens which afflict us, you come to our aid, and lift us up so that together we face life with renewed courage and strength.

False Guilt

God takes our sins farther away than the east is from the west. (Psalm 103:12)

When I was a young boy I had terrible nightmares. I saw myself in the dock in a large courtroom with everyone shouting, 'guilty, guilty', and pointing an accusing finger at me. I couldn't make out who they were or what they were accusing me of, but I was scared. I looked up at the Judge in his high chair with his red robes and long white wig – a frightening figure – as he peered at me over his glasses. I felt so lost, and I kept on crying out to him, 'not guilty, my Lord, not guilty'. It didn't seem to make any impact on him. He just kept staring at me. The nightmares have long since gone, but they are for many a reality which destroys their life. Because of *false guilt* their lives are a perpetual nightmare. Joan is a typical example of what I mean.

When I first met her she was in a terrible mess. She suffered from severe bouts of depression, and was fatalistic in her attitude to life. If the worst happened to her, it was, she considered, just what she deserved. She was both judge and jury in her own condemnation. The root cause of her trouble was that she was sexually abused by her uncle when she was only six years old, and would never forgive herself for that. It is relatively easy to forgive people who have wronged you, but it is practically impossible to forgive yourself if you suffer from false guilt. Here is how she describes her attitude.

'I have forgiven my uncle long ago because he was a weak man. He had too much to drink anyway, and probably didn't know what he was doing. Part of it must have been my fault, and I just cannot forgive myself. In fact I don't want to. I have never really prayed to God as someone who loves me because I know he just couldn't after what I have done. I don't love myself so why should he? I get terrible fits of depression when I think about it, and I would have committed suicide a long time ago but that would have been the easy way out. I have been in and out of psychiatric hospitals, but I wasn't cured mainly because I didn't want to be. My guilt was my punishment. As for the therapeutic value of marriage, who would want me anyway because I am soiled, and sex is a dirty thing. I have lost contact with my family and never visit my old home because of the hurtful memories it stirs up within me.'

It is hard-going trying to help Joan forgive herself, and be healed of her hurtful, destructive memories. She not only has a low opinion of herself, but looks on God as a vengeful judge. The nightmares I had as a child she still has today. The only trouble is that she pleads, 'guilty, guilty, my Lord'. Someday in her dreams and in reality I hope the judge will call, 'Silence in Court'. Then he will smile at her and say, 'I find no charge proved against you. You may leave the court a free person.' That day will come when she realizes that God is not a vengeful judge but a merciful Father who reassures her, 'not guilty, my child, not guilty'.

Father, you forgive me my sins because of the greatness and selflessness of your love for me as your child; teach me to concentrate more on your mercy and compassion as a Father than on my own sinfulness, and heal me of false guilt and memories of the past which cripple me, and prevent me from growing into the fully free person you would have me be.

Do Not Be Afraid

Why are you so frightened? How is it that you have no faith? (Mark 4:40)

I want to tell you about Jim. You probably rub shoulders with people like him every day of your life. He is a normal, nice-to-have-made-it, friendly person whom you would like to have as your next-door neighbour. In his mid-forties, he has a secure middle management job with all the perks that go with it. His wife, Debbie, is a wonderful, happy person, and he has three smashing children. They go to church every Sunday, so before God and man the future looks rosy. A perfect setting for domestic bliss? Well, not quite. Let me tell you a bit more.

Jim has been obsessed by all sorts of silly fears all his life. He is like so many people today. In recent years the pressure mounted until it was at breaking point. Debbie persuaded Jim to come to the services I conduct for inner healing. I'll let him take up the story.

'I lived in a cage of fear,' he wrote to me, 'ever since I can remember, and I was unable to break loose. Recently I have become more and more restless, and panic at the slightest thing.

'Fear became such a powerful force in my life that it warped my judgement of my business colleagues, my friends, and even of Debbie and the kids. I climbed into my fear capsule and refused to come out. It was my drug to which I had become addicted. At the first session I resolved not to come forward for healing. I felt great leaving the church because I had resisted the emotional pressure to conform. Yet once outside in the cold street I knew in my heart that it was fear which had really won.

'The next month was sheer hell. I could hardly wait for your next healing session. At the appropriate time I rushed forward for healing. You told me I was like an alcoholic asking for a cure while keeping a brandy bottle in his coat pocket just for safety. You said I had to lose my fear first. I hated you then. I was never so angry in all my life, but a few days later the light began to dawn. The next time I met you, you called me forward and asked Debbie and my family to pray over me. I felt a warmth within me thawing all the ice which chilled my inner being. I knew then that I was free and a new life had just begun.'

Today Jim, Debbie and the family are truly happy. He is a new person, the kind of person deep-down in his heart he always wanted to be. He had to come to terms with his fear. For Jim it was his faith in Christ which won through the storms of fear which battered him on all sides. He

has left behind the valley of the darkness of fear.
It was his faith which brought him peace.

*Father, take from us all those fears which burden
us and reduce life to a standstill, making us less
human, less free to be ourselves. Give us a faith
that conquers fear so that when fear knocks at our
door we may open it in faith knowing that there is
no one there.*

Little Children

I will not leave you orphans. Anybody who loves me will be loved by my Father. (John 14:18, 21)

I want to tell you about my friend Margaret. When she was only a few days old she was abandoned by her mother at the door of a local convent in Ireland. In those days, more than today, it was an intolerable social stigma to be an unmarried mother. When she was five, Margaret was adopted by an extremely loving couple who loved her as much as they did their own six children. Still, Margaret fretted about her real parents, and no matter how anyone tried to console her this gap in her life came between her and the rest of the family. She just did not feel she 'belonged'. She resented God for allowing her to be abandoned by her natural parents, and there was a part of her, deep-down inside, which no one could reach.

After leaving school she met and married Sean, a gentle, caring husband, and they were blessed with three lovely children. Loving and loved though she was, and Margaret was always a warm character, the nagging circumstances of her early childhood haunted many a waking moment. One day, as if by compulsion, she visited an orphanage where she saw a little baby, John, and in him she saw herself. Sean agreed to adopt him, and just as in her own case, John was loved by everyone in the family. Yet Margaret's hang-up remained, and her tension was affecting every aspect of her life. In desperation she, and the whole of the family, came to ask me and our ministry of healing team to pray for them. Here is how Margaret describes what happened.

'Soon after you laid your hands on my head, and I lay still with my eyes closed, I felt God's loving power within me. I knew I had not only to forgive my mother for abandoning me, and the father I never knew, but to love them as well, not only because they brought me into the world of my adopted parents, but because they must have been under all sorts of social pressures. I thanked God for my husband and children, especially little John. For the first time in my life I was experiencing a loving father in my life, and my prayers and tears began to flow. I could feel a cheek against mine, and little arms around my neck. When I opened my eyes I could see it was John telling me "I love you Mammy".'

John thought that his mother was ill when he saw her lying so still with her eyes closed. So he snatched himself away from those who were holding him, and threw himself on his mother in floods of child's tears. It moved us all, especially Sean and their three children. I stood back and watched the family embrace each other in a most beautiful, loving way. It was the little boy John who taught his mother that those who love us are really our brothers and sisters, our mother and father. It was Jesus who said of little children, 'of such is the Kingdom of Heaven'.

Father, you provided your Son Jesus with a loving home; bless all adopted children and those who provide them with a loving, caring family life. May the children be a source of happiness and fulfilment to their parents, and may the parents love and cherish the children as their very own.

Prejudices

The truth I have now come to realise,' said Peter, 'is that God does not have favourites.' (Acts 10:34)

The one tag we don't want attributed to us is the word 'prejudiced'. Yet we are all prejudiced to some degree. We may have biased, 'extra strong' views about coloured people, social classes or certain countries which lead us to write them off. But like most people I like to think that I am an open and fair-minded person. Yet I have preconceived judgements about people and institutions concerning which I know very little at first-hand, and I haven't taken the time to really find out the truth.

Take religion for example. In Ireland I grew up among Protestants, and many are still among my best friends today. And yet somehow subconsciously I felt they were different from us. They were by some strange quirk in my thinking identified with the remnants of British rule in Ireland. In a way they weren't Irish, and they didn't belong to the right Church anyway! *We* were the true Church, and therefore they were wrong. I never set foot inside a Protestant Church until long after I became a priest. *I was prejudiced*. I suppose Roger who was a Presbyterian minister in Northern Ireland was prejudiced too. When he wrote to me he said, 'I was quite content to live my life as a Protestant minister looking after my people while the Catholic priests looked after theirs. Deep-down, though I respected and even admired most of my Roman Catholic neighbours, I still felt they were not Christian. They were not Bible people with all this emphasis on the Pope and statues and things!

'My own people had suffered much at the hands of extreme nationalists until one day some extremists of my own people retaliated. They bombed the church of one of my Roman Catholic friends. I had to try to understand how he felt in his situation. It was a painful process because I felt in some way his people deserved it, and yet in my heart I knew he was a good priest and a reconciler if ever there was one. As we prayed together we realized how far apart we had grown in our denominations so that he was praying to a Catholic God and I to a Protestant God. Slowly we began to share our prejudices with each other, and now we try to lead our people into a new area of trust and mutual respect. We talk of the future together. We seek those things which unite rather than divide us, but we still have a long way to go.'

What we need is a change of attitude, a healing deep within us. As with Roger, so with us all. We all need healing of our prejudices and hatreds.

There can be no peace in our hearts until we try to be at peace with everyone. Jesus said we were to love not only our friends but our enemies as well. We will never do it unless we try to understand them and look at the world through their eyes, so that in time they can look at it through ours. We have to dislodge the bricks from the wall of prejudice, and together, on both sides, use them to build a bridge of peace.

Father, purify in me, and all the people of my country, our love for our nation. May our minds be like that of your Son Jesus Christ who knew what was good for the peace of his land and people, and may we strive by word and action to foster unity and peace among all our people whatever their social class or creed.

A Sense of Humour

God loves a cheerful giver. (2 Corinthians 9:7)

Fr John is one of my best friends. He is special because I believe that he has discovered the elusive secret of life and happiness. He is a sheer joy to be with. His peace and inner contentment flow out to everyone he meets, and yet his lifestyle is simple and uncomplicated. He is the same to rich and poor, the famous and the faceless because he is himself. Whether he's on the altar saying Mass or trying to sort out some bitter feud in his area, he is always at peace. His peace is within him, and how he needs it, because his parish is in the heart of strife-torn Belfast. He has known and shared the heartaches of his people. He has witnessed violence in some of its worst forms at first-hand level, and yet he has remained calm and cheerful. How does he do it?

One of his secrets is that he has a most wonderful sense of humour. There is no time in his day or life for bitterness or recrimination. He knows that if he took himself too seriously then he would become either depressed by what is going on round him, or fall into the trap of becoming sectarian and judgemental. Fr John is on God's side. His love knows no boundaries or barriers. And he often laughs quite hilariously when I get him to talk about himself. 'God had a fantastic sense of humour,' he said, 'when he sent me here. And so I leave him to show me what I must do. We all pretend to be better than we are, but I know myself for what I am – a very ordinary person trying to help people to make sense of their lives. And so I laugh through my tears, and trust in God's wisdom and mercy. If he can use me, he can use anyone.'

One day a self-righteous woman confronted Fr John in pharisaical anger. 'I don't come to your church,' she said as she wagged a threatening fist in his face, 'because it is full of hypocrites.' 'Don't exaggerate, my dear,' replied Fr John, tongue in cheek, 'it's not quite full. There's room for one more.' It is his sense of humour that has seen him through not only this little domestic encounter but through other situations when his life was in danger.

Fr John lives one day at a time. He leaves the past and the future to God. He can just about cope with the problems each day inevitably brings. He is his own man, living his life as best he can, not to please anyone else but God, whom he looks to as a Father. There are times when he has a good old tussle with God because he is always asking the question 'Why?' Somehow, sometimes, I think he gets the answer.

Fr John has brought peace to so many including myself that in his situation I think of the comforting words of Christ to his followers, 'You will be weeping and wailing while the world will rejoice; you will be sorrowful but your sorrow will turn to joy.' I think of Fr John and his advice to everyone: 'If you have nothing to smile about, then smile at yourself.' So why not try it? It works. At least it does for Fr John.

Father, when you created the world you wanted us to live in true happiness and to deal sensitively with each other. Give me a heart full of gratitude to you for all you have given to me, and a serenity which nothing can disturb, so that in my daily contact with others I may be to them a channel of your happiness, love, gentleness and joy.

Love Your Enemies

But I say this to you: love your enemies and pray for those who persecute you; in this way you will be sons of your Father in heaven. (Matthew 5:44)

'Love your enemies,' says Jesus. This seems a strange doctrine. It may sound all right for him but what about us poor mortals? As a teaching it's way up in the clouds, too idealistic, too divorced from reality. And yet there is something very special for everyone in his message if we really study its inner meaning.

I think the only way to understand 'loving your enemies' is to concentrate on 'love' and not 'enemies'. First of all, we have to love ourselves. If we don't love ourselves then we can't love God or anyone else, least of all our enemies. Hate ourselves, and we become our own worst enemy.

And we all have enemies whether we like it or not. People who don't like us for who or what we are, or what we say and do. Don't worry; we are in good company. Jesus, lovable though he was, had many enemies. The religious leaders, the Pharisees, didn't like what he said. They even criticized him for healing people on the Sabbath Day. Despite the dangers Jesus had to be true to himself. He refused to dilute his message. Like him we, too, have to be true to ourselves. We cannot remain silent or adopt false attitudes just for the sake of popularity.

The most difficult enemy to love and forgive is the one who destroys our inner peace of mind, the one whom we don't seem to be able to get out of our thoughts and emotions. I suffered like that for over two years. I was wounded deep inside by someone whose position gave him an advantage over me. I had got a thing about the way I had been treated. I talked it over endlessly with friends. I'm sure I bored them. No matter how I tried I could not come to terms with it. It began to affect my health. I often lay awake at night saying to myself, 'I hope he's not asleep. He couldn't be after all he's done to me.' But it was I who was awake while he slept soundly.

I prayed for healing from the hurt which was growing deep inside me, like a cancer destroying me. Then through prayer, and the help of a wonderful person, I made a resolution to let the past die. I wrote to my 'enemy' and told him that in my heart I wished him well. As I wrote the darkness lifted from me, and I felt gloriously free, like an eagle set free from its cage flying away to a new life.

So I think I know a little more now about what 'loving' enemies really means. Surely it is being at peace within ourselves and forgiving those who hurt us. Wishing them well in their life and wishing them happiness. In this way we discover a new dimension to love. That love that sets us free.

Father, your Son Jesus Christ on the cross forgave those who condemned and crucified him. Fill our minds and hearts today with forgiveness for those nearest and dearest to us who have crushed our spirit in any way by their words, actions or attitude so that we may be free to praise you, with unfettered spirit, who has already forgiven us. May we dwell on your love rather than our own hurt, and like Jesus on the cross may all our pain be swallowed up in Christ's resurrection.

Famine

Jesus said to his disciples, 'I feel sorry for all these people. They have nothing to eat.' (Mark 8:2)

Famine is a reality which is part of the world in which we live. We have all seen emaciated children staring at us with their big eyes from our television screens. And yet in a world of plenty we feel powerless to help them.

I know personally about famine because I was privileged to help in a desperate situation. I was in Africa many years ago giving lectures and sermons when I was told about a famine which had broken out about two hundred miles away. A convoy of food was hurriedly arranged by the priests and nuns. We arrived at our destination late at night.

We started the distribution of food at crack of dawn. I shall never forget the sight that met my eyes. There were literally thousands of people in never-ending queues waiting for food. They were quiet – frighteningly so. It was like watching half-dead people from whom life expectancy and hope had been completely drained by the events which all too often had become the pattern of their lives. They had neither the strength nor inclination to protest. No need here for the police or army to keep them under control.

One by one they came to receive their ration of food. I couldn't take my eyes off them. They seemed so patient. The sadness and cruelty of it all overpowered me. After five hours standing in what had now become the punishing noonday sun I began to feel tired. But what of them? Rather ashamedly I carried on. A young mother was next in the queue. Even though she looked a girl herself she had four very young children with her, one a tiny baby on her back. Before she held out her bowl for food she curtsied to me, a gesture of thanks for bringing food for herself and her children. When I filled her bowl with the precious maize she just stood there, closed her eyes, and made the sign of the cross, very slowly and reverently. I asked her through an interpreter why she did it. 'I am a Christian,' she said, 'and the first thing I want to do is to thank God my Father for providing food for my family.' In the face of such simple faith I fought hard to keep back the tears. She looked so frail and yet so nobly serene. Slowly she turned away with her children. I paused for what seemed like an eternity to let the message in all its beauty sink into my soul.

I shall probably never meet the young African mother again, but the memory of her peace and dignity will never leave me. She made me realize that despite the most horrendous circumstances faith can still shine through. She has really taught me that all of us need to be thankful for what we have received of food, drink, health, family and friends. And to be prepared to share with others. Jesus said, 'It is for you to give them to eat.' I shared a bowl of maize with my African sister. She shared with me her gratitude to God and her faith. In the sharing it was I, as much as she, who was hungry and needed to be helped.

Heavenly Father, you have provided sufficient food for all the people of our world, and when disaster strikes, leaving many people dying of hunger, we become more aware of our common humanity and our obligation to feed them. Open our hearts to the poor and underprivileged; may we make them our special friends because in our sharing bread with them we become aware of our deep spiritual needs. Help us to do always all we can to relieve the spiritual hunger of those around us because man cannot live on bread alone.

The Dynamo of Love

I give you a new commandment: love one another; just as I have loved you. (John 13:34)

I want to write about love – love for each other and for God. As the years roll by I have become more and more aware of God the Father's love for me. It colours my whole attitude to life. I get hundreds of letters from people who are unhappy and depressed. They seem to have no purpose in their lives. For them life is loveless and barren. They never experience true love. Never reach out to anyone other than themselves.

Such a person was Joan. She grew up in a family where there was little or no outward expression of love. She knew from the very tender age of three or four that her parents were different from most other parents. They didn't seem to love each other, and certainly didn't love her. They were good parents in the sense that they provided for all her material needs, but that was as far as it went. When Joan reached out to them for something more – for love – there was no response. The line was dead.

Then along came Jim. He loved Joan even

when she was unable to return his love. For the first few months, and even years, he received an emotional battering. No matter how hard he tried to share his love for her she instinctively put up barriers. This was the only language she knew. One day it dawned on her, not only that she was hurting Jim, but that he really cared for her as if she were part of himself. Within months she became a changed person. 'For the first time in my life,' she said, 'I knew what love really meant. It frightened me at first and then gradually, through Jim's help, I allowed it to soak into my life. It has changed my whole attitude.'

The reason for Joan's initial loneliness, and that of so many other people, is that deep inside each one of us there is a power created for love. It is hidden in the inner recesses of our personality. I call it the powerhouse of life and love. Many people lock the door which leads to that inner powerhouse, and so for them the great dynamo of love never comes to life. They are never alight within themselves, and so make do with candles. It needs someone other than ourselves to set that dynamo in action. It was Jim, her loving husband, who turned on the switch of *light* which love brought into Joan's life.

Jim is also a devout Christian. Joan came with him to church regularly, and one day she heard the priest talking of God the Father's love for us. It clicked with her; 'I knew suddenly, as if in a flash,' said Joan, 'that my love for Jim and his love for me were all part of God's love for us, and for everyone. Jim was the human contact God used to make me come alive in human love. Jesus is my contact with God the Father to make me aware of a deeper love.'

I believe that we all can help each other to set the dynamo of love in action if we really care about each other. Jesus said, 'I stand at the door and knock. If anyone opens to me I will come in and make my home there.' The door is the door to the human heart. It can only be opened from inside. So why not take a risk and open your life to love, and to God who loves you as a Father, even when you don't love yourself?

Father, fill us with an awareness of your unique love for us, so that we may always open the door of our hearts to all those who need our love and friendship, and by our contact with them may we help them to come alive, and find a true purpose in life.

Animals are Friends

They took the colt to Jesus and threw their cloaks on its back. (Mark 11:7)

Like the vast majority of people, I love animals. They have played a great part in my life. Ever since the age of three I have had a dog as a pet. And each one has been different. Each had its own special characteristics and meant a lot to me at various times in my life, but none more so than 'Pax'.

'Pax', the Latin word for 'peace', was a Red Setter given to me sixteen years ago, and we have been through many ups and downs together. She was very sensitive, knew my mood, sensed what I was thinking. In 1977, for instance, I was heavily involved in the Peace Movement in Northern Ireland. I went to Belfast for some important meetings; while I was there the La Mon Restaurant was blown up, killing thirteen people. I went to the scene of the tragedy, saw the bodies horribly disfigured by the fire, and it had a devastating effect on me. When I came back home to Yorkshire, I could not eat for nearly three weeks. My secretary scolded me. 'Look at Pax,' she said, 'she is wasting away because of you. She refuses to eat anything, so snap out of it and take your food.' I did just that, and in a few minutes Pax went to her bowl looking for hers. Who said that dogs are just dumb animals!

But the great thing in Pax's life was the one and only time she had puppies. I thought it was a good thing for her to have a *small litter*. Bring out the motherly instinct in her. So, accordingly, she mated, and the local vet said she would be the proud mother of about seven puppies. How wrong he was. One Wednesday afternoon she started delivering her offspring. The first batch of eight arrived pretty promptly followed by four more at infrequent intervals. By midnight she had delivered fourteen pups, so all the community went to bed feeling very happy. Two of our nuns stayed behind to look after Pax and her puppies. When I came down in the morning she had delivered six more, and while we were at Mass, she produced another two, bringing her final total to twenty-two (fifteen of whom survived). A world record. So today she is in the *Guinness Book of Records*. She turned the whole centre upside down. We had to get a foster mother for some of her pups. For six weeks, we all became 'canine midwives'. Pax and family starred in 'Blue Peter', 'Nationwide', and the national press. People came from far and wide to see her and her family. The way she protected and nourished her puppies gave me deep insights into what being a mother is all about.

But above all, Pax loved people. She didn't

care who they were. They got a whack from her tail, and a generous welcoming lick. In her own way she helped people in our centre, people who came to us often because they had problems. There were many like Tom. He was withdrawing from drugs and no one could get through to him. One day, I sent him off with Pax for a walk in the woods. When he came back, he was a changed man. Pax had licked him into shape. 'She is the first living thing in months,' he said, 'that showed me such generous affection. I meant something to her. So there must be some good in me.'

Pax died nearly four years ago. How I missed her. Today I have another Red Setter, also called Pax, and she too is unique. When we love and see animals as our friends in the world we share together, we might come close to the mind of Jesus Christ who spoke so lovingly about the birds of the air, and was carried into Jerusalem on the back of a donkey. He showed our need of animals. Thank God for the pets in our homes who give us such joy and comfort. Like Pax they were meant to bring us peace.

Father, your Son Jesus chose a donkey to carry him into his beloved Jerusalem; may we in our journey through life look upon animals as our companions and your gift to us as together, man and beast, we share the beauty of your creation and love.

Be Glad You're You

Every hair on your head has been counted . . .
you are worth more than hundreds of sparrows.
(Luke 12:7)

Strange as it may seem, one of the most difficult
things to do in life is to be glad that you are you.
To accept yourself. Most people don't. They wish
they were someone else, living a different kind
of life. They envy others more fortunate than
themselves. And yet the joy of being alive, and
of being yourself, is the secret of all true happiness. This is very much in line with the teaching
of Christ, who in Luke chapter 4, verse 18, said
he had come to set the prisoners free. And we
are prisoners, because we fail to live the kind of
life that God our Father wants us to live. We are
prisoners of a world that wants us to conform to
what people expect us to be. A world that does
not want us to be ourselves. So Christ's gospel
releases us from within. Sets us free.

Free for what? Free to be yourself so that, no
matter what happens, you are still glad that you
are who you are. And this gladness comes from
deep inside yourself. It is nothing to do with riches

or fame, or the result of arrogance, or self-deception. It is being at peace within yourself because of your awareness that you are unique, and that your life has a purpose.

Such a person was my friend the Carmelite nun, Mother St John. She certainly was unique. I never met anyone quite like her in my life. She was a really happy person, and she shared her happiness with everyone she met. It didn't matter if people were rich or poor, Catholic or Protestant, or no religion at all. Mother St John treated them all the same. To her they were individuals, each in his own right. And she could do this out of the fullness of her own personality. She certainly knew who she was, and people who met her dropped their masks and became themselves, many for the first time.

Even though she lived a so-called sheltered life, she had an uncanny knack of knowing what other people were going through. And very few were as compassionate and understanding as she was with those who had problems. People from all walks of life sought her out, not only for advice, but just to be in her presence. They could relax and be themselves with her. Born in the last century she lived very much in this. She never recalled the past with nostalgia or regret. Neither did she speculate about the future. 'Life,' she often told me with a smile, 'comes moment by moment, and we mustn't waste it. It's too precious.' She was fasincated by everything around her. I remember the cast of 'Jesus Christ Superstar' in the early seventies coming to sing selections of their modern musical at our conference centre. Mother St John was engrossed not only in the music, but in the young artistes with their way-out clothes. You could hear their laughter ringing out from the guest-room where they met her. One of them summed her up for me: 'Isn't she wonderful? Isn't she a real person?'

Mother St John wasn't a carbon-copy, typical Carmelite nun. She was a most lovable person because she was herself, who happened also to be an excellent nun. Nothing overshadowed her personality. You might say it was easy for her because she was protected in a convent. But in many subtle ways convents and other institutions tend to stylize people. They become institutionalized. And yet we were all meant to be free, to be real persons. But it isn't easy. Why? Because we are conditioned on all sides not to be ourselves. And so we change our image and our lifestyle so that we can be accepted. And all the laughter, the gladness of being who we are, goes out of our lives. We become faceless people who have lost the capacity to laugh at ourselves, and our sometimes crazy world. So every morning when you get up and look at yourself in the mirror, be happy. You may not like what you see. Here, you may think, is no work of art! But cheer up, God doesn't judge you by your face. He reads your heart, what's within you. His love will change what needs to be changed. And he will set you really free to be yourself. Give yourself a treat. Celebrate yourself. God loves you even if you don't particularly love yourself. And isn't that a reason to be glad that you are you?

Father, whose mercy is boundless and whose gifts are without end, give us the courage to be ourselves and make us truly grateful that you have made us as we are. What is wrong in us you will change, and whatever is good in us you will perfect, and for this we praise and thank you.

Inner Strength

Come to me, all you who labour and are over-burdened, and I will give you rest. (Matthew 11:28)

We are all afraid of suffering. And why shouldn't we be? Even Jesus himself on the night before he died prayed, 'Father, if it be possible, let this suffering pass me by.' I have a word for all those who are suffering from some apparently terminal disease, especially cancer. I am sure the story about Jo will give you hope and bring you inner peace and strength.

Jo is a very sensitive, artistic person, easily hurt. She has not had an easy life. She was married in 1965, and seven years later her husband walked out on her, leaving her with two small daughters. Unable to afford to keep her home going she was forced to live in a tenement where, she told me: 'I had to get used to the bad language, the graffiti, having milk bottles thrown at me. The man next door committed murder by throwing someone over the railings into the yard below. His wife threatened me with a knife, and I was frightened but I tried not to show it. After seven years of this I had a nervous breakdown and then found a lump in my breast, which led to a mastectomy. I believe my cancer was caused by stress.

'I came to your healing service last year. Although I was a Christian, I was a Christian very much in need of inner healing. When you laid your hands on my head I felt all the pain and horror leave me, and the shattering memories of all those years of living in a tenement simply evaporated. Nowadays I am better equipped than ever before to cope with life. I have an inner strength which is unbelievable. I can even look upon my disease as a power for good because it enables me to talk to and help other people who have cancer. I know I can help them and that helps me.

'My doctors think I am a new person. I know I am. Whatever happens to me in the future, I believe I shall never lose my inner peace. My stress has gone and I bear no grudge against anyone. I still suffer from cancer. Of course I want to be completely, physically healed, but I just leave that, as I do the rest of my life, in God's hands. The main thing is that I am at peace within myself, and live each day to the full.'

There are many Jo's in today's world, people who cope with the most frightening odds. But deep inside them there is a peace which is the stuff of which heroism is made. In Jo's case the source of this peace is her belief in God the Father's love for her. 'I give each day to him,' she said, 'and he fills it for me with his peace and strength.' On the cross as he lay dying, Christ gave his life to his Father, 'Father into your hands

I commit my spirit.' For him there was no more fear, only peace and forgiveness. May all of you reading this, who are fighting cancer or any other disease, find inner peace. May you lose your fear. Remember Jo and Psalm 23: 'Though I walk in the valley of darkness no evil will I fear. You are there with your crook and your staff; with these you give me comfort.'

Father, you do not protect us against suffering, but when we seem to be at the end of our reserves, and darkness seems to engulf us, you give us an inner strength, light, and peace through which we know you have been with us all the time, even in our darkest hours.

Wrappings

God does not see as man sees; man looks at appearances but God looks at the heart. (1 Samuel 16:7)

Most of us think we know ourselves pretty well. We are, or seem to be, quite sure of our likes and dislikes. Yet it is only when we come up against an unexpected situation that we really discover just what our true feelings are. Often they are the opposite of what we believed about ourselves. The best way to show you what I mean is to tell you a story about a friend of mine, Basil, and how he discovered himself, his likes and dislikes, through an unexpected situation.

Basil has been a friend of mine for over twenty years. He is in every sense of the word an upright, open-minded man who believes in fair play for everyone whatever their race, colour or creed. If he is intolerant about anything then it is about prejudice! He has never been afraid to stand up and be counted for what he believes in. Often I have heard him speak at meetings where his views ran contrary to popular opinion. And yet he expressed those views so sincerely, clearly and

99

quietly that everyone admired him. Everyone, that is, except the people who were way over the top in their own personal views. And his great crusade in life was for justice and peace. It was *the* big thing in his life.

He was a Third World man through and through. He spent all his free time befriending immigrants to this country, as well as campaigning for the release of political prisoners. His study was filled with photographs of his heroes in far-off countries, kept in captivity for their beliefs. He knew all about each one of them, how long they were imprisoned, what they had suffered, what happened to their families and so on.

Basil himself was a great family man. Nigel, his eldest son, was the apple of his eye. In a sense the son was overshadowed, even a little daunted, by his father's attitude and standing in the community. As usually happens in such cases he tended to be very shy and retiring. When the time came for him to go to boarding school to study for his 'A' levels, his father was apprehensive lest he might fall in with the wrong company. What a joy it was to him when Nigel wrote to say that almost immediately he had made a very special friend, David. It was soon obvious from his letters that David was a highly talented, artistic young student who had a very positive influence on Nigel, encouraging him in his studies as well as widening his appreciation of the arts. But the great bonus as far as Basil was concerned was that David shared his own crusading passion for justice and peace. Basil could hardly wait to meet his son's new-found friend.

And as usually happens with friends at boarding school David was invited to spend a long weekend at Nigel's home. When Basil went to meet them at the station he was all smiles in anticipation of at last meeting his son's best friend, about whom he had heard so much. The smile soon froze when David stepped off the train. He was black. Basil's reaction was completely out of character. The atmosphere of the welcome froze. It was, to put it mildly, a highly embarrassing situation. Basil drove them home in silence, and when David went to his room he told Nigel off in no uncertain manner. 'You should have told us what he was,' he said angrily, 'so that we could have been prepared for this.' Nigel said nothing.

Eventually Basil calmed down sufficiently after dinner to allow him to show David round the house. When they came to the study David noticed a poster on the wall of a political prisoner for whose freedom Basil had been campaigning for years. 'That's my father,' said David. 'Thank you for helping him. He needs people like you to help him to keep going in prison.' Basil fell silent. After all, what could he say? The unexpected situation, the black skin of his son's best friend, brought home to him perhaps for the first time, his own inner, deep-seated prejudices. Was he really completely for justice and peace for all no matter the cost? I wonder.

We often wrap ourselves in self-righteousness and do-gooding until the problem comes to our own front door. That's when we have to live up to the ideals we expect of others; when we have to overcome our own prejudices and see beyond the externals, the wrappings. God's Son might have come as a mighty king, and people might have followed him because of his power. But he didn't. He came as a baby wrapped in swaddling clothes, and his palace was a stable. Most people round him never got past the wrapping. But a few did, and they really knew him for who and what he was.

Father, you sent your Son Jesus on earth in human form, and many who met him could not look beyond the fact that he came from Nazareth. Teach me to see beyond the human wrappings of those I meet, and, while stripping me of my prejudices, clothe them in the beauty of your loving self in whose image we are all made.

Nature

God said, 'Let the earth produce every kind of living creature.' And so it was. God saw all he had made, and indeed it was very good. (Genesis 1:24, 31)

I want to share with you a few thoughts on the beauty of nature in the world around us if only we took time to appreciate it. Jesus did. He saw the wild flowers of the field as being far more beautiful than King Solomon in all his finest regal robes.

To be a Christian is to listen to nature and understand what God is saying to us through it. Nature has always spoken to me and been a great source of my deep inner peace. Whenever I find myself in a stressful situation nature seems to echo a sympathetic response and soothes me like ointment.

One day a few weeks ago, a day that was filled with stories of violence and stress, I went out in the garden just as the evening shadows were beginning to fall. My thoughts were filled with sadness and despair at what was happening in the world around me. Then I heard a bird sing. As it poured out its song above my head I listened to a sound far sweeter than even the most delicate instrument could ever produce. Then its song was taken up by other birds in the nearby bushes and trees as if nature in a huge orchestra had been waiting for me to appear. The sound penetrated my whole being. I stood still. I felt as if I were in another world, a world of beauty and hope. This peace flowed over me like clear, refreshing water. Then the singing of the birds reached a crescendo and stopped just as suddenly as it began. I stayed there, I don't know how long, but I knew that out there in the gathering dusk were my friends who filled my soul with peace and hope. Have you ever heard the birds' evensong? I have heard it many times before, and each one touches me with a beauty as if I were hearing it for the first time.

In our concrete jungle I'm very fortunate because I have a garden. At the moment it is full of colour and brightness. The brave snowdrops which defied the winter have given way to masses of daffodils and other beautiful spring flowers. I am continually in awe at the extraordinary variety of little wild flowers which seem to come from nowhere and which peep impishly through the fallen leaves and dead wood of winter.

Nature in birds and flowers speaks to me of life and hope. And I want others to share it with me. I feel sad for those who are deprived of this beauty because of their surroundings, or their busy, hectic life. Perhaps we might take more time to listen to a bird singing, or to look at a flower or at a tree beginning to rouse itself from the long sleep of winter. They will lift us up, and fill us with a peace which we need and which no one should disturb. They help us to make sense of our noisy, disturbed world.

Father, slow me down so that I may take time to look at a flower and see its fragile beauty, to admire the majesty of a towering oak tree, to feast my eyes on a dawn that heralds a new day or a flaming sunset which draws it to its close. May I listen to the birds as they sing to your glory so that in all of your creation which you saw was good, my spirit may be refreshed so that I too be lifted up to share in beholding the beauty all around me, and to praise and thank you with a song in my heart.

Resurrection

If Christ has not been raised then our preaching is useless and your believing it is useless. (1 Corinthians 15:14)

Like most people, when I was young I was inclined to make infallible judgements on almost everything. Instant wisdom was never far away. But as I have grown older I have become less and less certain about many things, and more and more convinced about a few beliefs which are very much part of me. Without them my life would not be worth living. And top of the list is my unshakeable belief in the resurrection of Jesus Christ from the dead. He said, 'I am the Resurrection and the Life,' and that he would rise from the dead. And he did just that. How he did it, or what kind of resurrection it was, doesn't worry me. I know, believe, deep inside me that Jesus is alive today and that he has conquered death. And his new life is my guarantee, hope, of life after death.

But I didn't always think or believe like that. At school I rarely thought about the resurrection. I said I believed in it because that was what my parents and teachers expected me to say. But I didn't really believe in it, I suppose, because in fact I never gave it much thought. For me Easter was a season of chocolate eggs and daffodils and holidays from school. That's all Easter meant to me.

Now all that has changed dramatically for me; especially over the past fifteen years since I committed my life totally to working for peace and inner healing. Now I know, in a way which I cannot properly put into words, the power of the risen Christ's living presence in our world. I have seen him change people's lives completely by the power of his resurrection so that those who seemed beaten by life have become new people with a completely new outlook and purpose.

I believe God the Father raised his Son from the dead in a way which neither I nor anyone else will ever fully understand, and in a sense it is foolish to try. For me personally Jesus walked out of the tomb with a new life which he wanted to share. His resurrection is the source of my strength, my belief, my life. When I minister inner healing in his name and resurrection I do so because this is what he would want me to do. And the power of the resurrection has dominated my whole way of thinking and acting. There is no situation, no person, outside the scope of the new life, which the risen Christ offers to people in our world.

The resurrection for me is not just the physical resurrection of Jesus from the dead, but is also, and much more so, the power that this brings to

107

his Church. No alcoholic, no depressed person, no drug addict or drop-out, no one in need of help and healing is excluded from the light and power of the person who on Easter Sunday morning walked through a garden of tombstones into a dying world which needed healing.

It was in his risen name that Peter said to the cripple who asked for money, 'Silver and gold I have none, but what I have I give thee. In the name of Jesus of Nazareth, rise up and walk.' And the man rose up and walked. That's what the resurrection means. People, though crippled in many ways, find new power and life through the name of the risen Christ. They walk in the light, and follow his footsteps into the new life of wholeness and peace.

Heavenly Father, I believe in the life, death and resurrection of your Son Jesus Christ, and that in his resurrection is my hope of one day being with you and all those whom I love in my earthly pilgrimage. Lift me up beyond the doubts and sorrows that cloud my vision so that in faith I may see more clearly the dawn of a new life with those I love, which will never end.

Suffering and Life

A woman in childbirth suffers, because her time has come; but when she has given birth to the child she forgets the suffering in her joy that a man has been born into the world. (John 16:21)

There is no escaping suffering. It is part and parcel of life. Jesus said, 'If anyone wants to be a follower of mine he must take up his cross daily and follow me.' (Matthew 16:24) And yet suffering is hard to bear.

I have always found it difficult to explain, even accept, suffering, not so much in my own life but in the lives of others who, through no fault of their own, have such terrible burdens to bear. I often ask why, and don't necessarily always come up with an answer. I hate mouthing platitudes that help no one. I believe most strongly that suffering taken in isolation is destructive unless we can see within it the germs of life and hope. Let me tell you a true story of new life that came out of suffering in the most appalling conditions.

Marie was a parishioner of mine in my first parish in the early fifties. She was a very private, shy person who kept herself and her six-year old son to themselves. All anyone seemed to know about her was that she was Polish and a war widow. Small in stature, one sensed an inner dignity and strength within her which could only come from some deep personal experience. One Sunday morning after Mass she came to see me and asked me to remember her late husband, Stefan, in my prayers. I sensed that she wanted to talk about him, and so I encouraged her to tell me her story.

'Stefan and I,' she said, 'were very much in love. We planned to marry when the war was over. Stefan was an idealist who loved his country. So it was inevitable that he would get involved in the resistance movement. He lived each day more dangerously, and so we decided to get married. It seemed pointless to wait any longer. Within three months Stefan was killed and I was in a concentration camp.

'The conditions there were indescribable. I could see that many people had, in their despair, given up the struggle for life. What kept me going was the movement of new life within me. I was bearing Stefan's child and mine. Despite the stench and the unbelievable human suffering all around me, I knew that each day brought the birth of our child that much nearer. The life within me kept me alive. And so my young son, Stefan, was born, and I knew that all the suffering of the concentration camp and the pain of childbirth were as nothing compared to the joy I felt when I held my baby in my arms for the first time. He was Stefan come to life again. My baby was my new life, and my new Poland.'

Now that story, while set in the most horrendous conditions of suffering has, I believe, within it the germs of life and hope. Today Marie lives a very happy and contented life in the south of England. Stefan is very happily married and a source of great joy to her. In them perhaps we see the setting, not only for what the Church calls Holy Week, but for our whole lives. We remember the shameful trial of Jesus, the cruelty of the soldiers, the desertion by his friends, and his painful death on the cross. Why all this suffering?

Even Jesus himself prayed that it would pass him by. But it was not to be. I can't really explain the death of Jesus in human terms, but I do know that in some mysterious way new life and hope were born on his cross. When he rose from the dead, Jesus walked the morning air bringing to everyone who believes in him new life and hope. To those of you who are weighed down by suffering, then my prayer is that you will find today, and every day, new life and hope, and the inner peace of Easter.

Father, pain ceases to be barren pain when in faith we believe that you are working through it mysteriously so that we may grow as persons, and be filled with hope such as a woman has who in joy gives birth to her child. In all the trials and injustices of life may we believe that you are in our pain, transforming it through hope into joy, and giving

111

us the strength to overcome all the burdens which would be too difficult for our human frailty to carry alone.

Words with Meaning

Out of the abundance of the heart, the mouth speaks. (Luke 6:45)

We often use words without giving them their full value or meaning. Why? Because we have not *experienced* in our own lives what they really mean. It is easy to talk about poverty when you are *rich*. Jesus not only talked about poverty; he was poor. What he did gave meaning to what he said. And his listeners who flocked to him in their thousands knew it. 'No one spoke as he does,' they said. 'He speaks with authority.'

Small wonder that I hate clichés or nice sounding empty phrases, especially in religion. They switch me off. I need to hear living words from a real person. For example, the word 'poverty' coming from the lips of Mother Teresa makes sense to me.

For many years I was adviser to a very popular Sunday evening religious television programme. It had a high-rating figure, and many famous people from all walks of life wanted to appear on it. Often the words of the readings or prayers they chose just did not ring true. I was quite dismayed,

113

therefore, when I discovered from the script that a famous Hollywood megastar had chosen as his reading Psalm 23, 'The Lord is my Shepherd'.

I had my doubts about James Stewart reading Psalm 23 in the electronically geared soulless atmosphere of a television studio. I asked him why he had chosen it, and if it meant anything to him. He answered quite simply: 'Everything. It is my favourite prayer because it supported myself and my wife in the saddest moment of our lives. It has become for us both *our prayer*. You see, knowing the Vietnam war would soon end we were both looking forward to our son's return home. He was a pilot in the US Air Force. Then two days before hostilities ceased we got word that our son had been shot down and killed. It seemed such a waste of a life. We were devastated. Letters of sympathy came pouring in from all over the world. Among them was one from a lady with her version of Psalm 23 which she thought would comfort us. That is the version I am reading today. My wife and I have *experienced* its power in our own lives.'

James Stewart began to read the psalm in front of the camera, and immediately I knew this was different. This was not acting. This was for real. His voice spoke not words but a cry from the heart. He read it so movingly that even when the cameras stopped turning everyone remained silent. The words seemed to speak to us all. Psalm 23 took on a new dimension in Studio 4 that day. It would never be the same again for many of us.

Perhaps you might like to read again and pray

Psalm 23. The pastures are not always green because life has many cruel twists and turns. Sometimes we seem to be surrounded by a harsh never-ending desert of sadness and loneliness. It is at times like these that we need to feel that the Lord is our Shepherd. That he is near even in the midst of our pain. Then the words of the psalm will come true for us. It will become our prayer. We will trust God even in sorrow.

So where he leadeth I can safely go
And in the blest hereafter I shall know
Why in His wisdom He hath led me so.

Father, the words of the Bible are so alive and personal that each person sees in them what he needs and loves as they speak to him of what lies deep in his heart; may we come to the Bible in every situation in our lives, and discover there the words of life which will soothe our pain, and make us more open and aware of your abiding and unchanging love for us.

Learning to Forgive

Forgive us our trespasses as we forgive those who trespass against us. (Matthew 6:12)

Remembrance Sunday is a very emotional day which affects people differently.

The most poignant moment for me is the two-minute silence in the Mall on Sunday. In that silence I can hear the muffled pain and cries for help of all the wounded of the two world wars. I always say a silent prayer for all those who have died, and I pray for an end to war.

One of those who always watches on television is Bob. His feelings, though mellowed by the years, still hurt. He was a prisoner of war for three years in a Japanese labour camp. Even today he finds it hard to forgive the soldiers who made him, and the other prisoners, suffer so cruelly. 'Over the years,' he told me, 'I have tried to blot out of my mind the things that happened in that camp. But I just can't. Many times I wake up in the night in a cold sweat. And for days afterwards I am filled with fear that it is all happening again. No one really knows what I feel. My life was destroyed in that camp. Every Remembrance

Sunday I think of all my mates, ordinary blokes like myself, who never made it home. Perhaps they were the lucky ones.'

Sounds hard, but then Bob is a very sick man. For years he has suffered the after-effects of the malnutrition and of the ill-treatment he received, so he is not likely to forget the last world war. Is he bitter? 'Sometimes,' he says, 'I just can't help it. I feel angry deep inside when I remember the cruelty which was all so unnecessary, and ruined so many lives. When I talk about it I am inclined to get bitter so I prefer not to talk about it at all.'

Bob comes to church every Sunday, so does he forgive? 'I try to,' he says. 'I say to myself that I have to because I'm a Christian, but I still find it hard. Jesus said we were to forgive our enemies. And he did when he said, "Father forgive them for they know not what they do." But I'm still trying. I hope I forgive them. I try not to blame them for what happened. But it's still hard.'

Bob is, for me, a sincere Christian. He knows forgiveness is a slow process because his memories still hurt him deep inside. 'To try to forgive' is a much more honest statement than to say that you forgive because that is what is expected of you. He is trying, and that is the main thing. I have prayed with him many times for the healing of his memories. At these sessions he gets great comfort and relief. But the healing of memories is a long and painful process. Apart from Bob there are millions of people in this country who have memories of childhood or events in their lives which cause them heartbreak, and even bitterness. So

117

long as we keep on trying to forgive, then we are doing what Jesus said: 'Love your enemies. Forgive them the wrongs they have done you. Your Father in Heaven has forgiven you.'

'Father, through the suffering, death and resurrection of your only Son Jesus Christ, you have forgiven all our sins; soothe our memories so that they may not dwell on the wrong people have done us in the past, but concentrate rather on your loving mercy which forgives everyone, including ourselves, because you are Lord and Father of all.

The Path to Faith

I bless you, Father, for hiding these things from the learned and the clever and revealing them to mere children. (Luke 10:2)

I wonder how many people reading this really believe in God. To say you believe in God is something very personal. It is something that most people don't like to talk about. And yet for me, my idea of God colours my whole attitude to life. And I want to write about it as openly as possible.

But the language of faith is a very difficult one. And very few people speak the same language. Our idea of God is coloured by so many hidden influences. And I often question why I believe the way I do while many others better than me do not. Or at least they say they don't. The path to faith is a very strange one. No two people come to believe in God in identical ways. Yet we generally come to a living experience of God through people.

The story of Harry's conversion is a typical example of what I mean. Harry married my sister, Mary, who was a very devout Christian. She dearly wanted Harry to share her faith, but she wanted him to do it his way, and in his time. She brought no undue pressure to bear on him. But it's not very easy to be an atheist or an agnostic if you have a priest as your brother-in-law!

In due course they came to Rome on a holiday. I was teaching there at the time, so I exposed Harry to all the colourful splendour of the Vatican. I even arranged a special audience for himself and Mary with Pope John XXIII, whom the world knew as Good Pope John. Harry thought he was a very kind, gentle old man, but that was as far as his conversion went. The path to Rome was not for him a pilgrimage of faith. I showed him round many beautiful churches and he met highly intelligent and understanding priests, but there was no flicker of heavenly response in Harry's eyes or heart. Much to Mary's regret Rome did not produce the result for which she had prayed and hoped.

It was Mary's ambition to go to Lourdes. She persuaded Harry to take me along, and so we went to spend a few days at this world-famous place of pilgrimage. Harry was quite appalled at the commercialism in the town of Lourdes itself. But when we went to the grotto the whole atmosphere changed. There he saw hundreds of sick people and their helpers praying silently. It was a different world. Something that Harry had never experienced before. He didn't pray. He just sat there on a bench, and gazed, not in a sense of curiosity, but of wonder. The night before we left Lourdes Harry disappeared after dinner. In the early morning Mary and I found him at the grotto, not sitting on a bench, but on his knees praying. When he looked up and saw us I knew something had happened. Harry had changed. 'For the past three days,' he said, 'I have watched the sick and marvelled at their faith. Wherever I went in the town I saw this blind boy pushing his crippled companion in a wheelchair. They were each other's eyes and feet. Whenever I looked out of the hotel window I seemed to see them passing by on the street outside. So tonight after dinner when I saw them again I followed them to the grotto. As I watched them pray together I felt a longing to share their faith. I wanted to be like them, to be one of them.' So Harry's conversion began, not through splendour or intellectual discussion, but through simple faith and sharing.

So who has faith and who hasn't? Jesus said of the Roman Army sergeant, 'I have not found such faith in Israel.' And how do you come to believe? The light for Harry was the blind boy and the cripple who helped him on his path to faith. My prayer is that you may find God as someone very special to you in your life. And may God go with you.

Father, bless all those whose influence on our lives, often without their knowing it, has so affected us that our faith has been stirred, our hope renewed, and our love rekindled, so that through them we have turned to you as the one true God who in simple things and people holds our lives in the palm of your hand.

Sensitivity

Jesus said, 'Let the little children come to me; it is to such as these that the Kingdom of God belongs.' (Mark 10:14)

Being sensitive to the needs of others is an essential part of the Christian gospel. To forget yourself and to think of others. Christ was the most sensitive person in human history. He lived for others. He was aware of everyone's needs whether it was bread in the desert, wine at a wedding, healing of sickness or forgiveness of sins. And, like him, when we are aware of other people's needs, and do something about them, then the Christian gospel comes alive in our lives.

It came alive for me very powerfully earlier this year when I went to Corby in Northamptonshire on a mission of inner healing. As usual during these services I began with an explanation of what healing is all about. In the front row of the church there was a little boy with his back to me, and he was watching his mother intently as in sign language she communicated to him what I was saying. When I had finished he turned round, and I saw his face for the first time. He was massively disfigured, and the sight of his twisted face touched my heart.

With my support group I went to pray with him and his mother. Their love for each other was tangible. The little boy was deaf and dumb but he looked up at me with the most beautiful, trusting brown eyes I have ever seen. I knew that he was aware of my concern for him and his mother. After a while he took his mother's hand and mine in his. His touch was very, very special. Everyone near us experienced a very delicate sense of compassion and inner peace.

After a while I moved on down the church to pray with other people, only to find that many of them were over-concerned with their own needs. In situations like that I generally feel drained. Soon I was so tired that I went back to the sanctuary to pray for more strength and discernment. I sat on a chair and closed my eyes, and almost immediately I felt two little arms enfolding me, and a head resting gently on my chest, and snuggling up against me. Great peace and power flowed back into me, and I knew that here in my healing ministry I had experienced something unique. I wondered where this power came from, and so I opened my eyes to find it was my little friend who had left his mother's side and come into the sanctuary to be near me. He was deaf and dumb, and probably needed more help than anyone else in the church, yet here he was comforting me, sensitive to my needs. His sensitivity and concern showed in his eyes, and when I got up refreshed to continue my healing work a lovely smile crossed his face.

During the healing session I expected my help to come from the prayers of the people in the church, but it was the little boy who was the one who was really sensitive to my tiredness, and he did something about it. Do you remember the story of the Good Samaritan who looked after the injured stranger, or the woman at Jacob's well who gave Jesus a drink of water when he was thirsty? 'As long as you did it to one of the least of my brethren you did it to me.' I cannot remember the little boy's name in Corby, but I shall never forget his sensitive, caring brown eyes. It is often those who need help themselves who are the first to help others.

Heavenly Father, we pray for all who are handicapped in the race of life; grant that in our own health and comfort we may be sensitive to the sorrow and pain of those around us, and in sharing with them may we realize how handicapped we are and what a blessing and healing the handicapped are to us in our lives.

Great Ordinary People

Happy the gentle: they shall have the earth for their heritage. (Matthew 5:4)

Children know how to be happy. They have the secret of life. I have known many wealthy people who seem to have everything going for them. They are short of nothing that money can buy. And yet so many of them are not happy because they lack deep inner peace. On the other hand I have met ordinary people doing ordinary jobs who are really happy because they are at peace within themselves, with God and their neighbour. They have discovered the secret of life. They are what I call the 'great ordinary people'. Let me tell you about one of them, John.

I was in charge of a Christian conference centre in Yorkshire and every so often we would help someone who came in off the roads to rehabilitate themselves. After a few months, we hoped, they left us refreshed and able to cope with life more fully and peacefully. John came to us at first for a few weeks to do some garden therapy for his nerves, but actually stayed with us for many years as part and parcel of our lives.

He was a very shy, truly Christian gentleman whose ever-present smile made up for his lack of conversation. People called him the 'gentle giant'. He was six feet four inches tall and built in proportion. When he came to us at first he was very withdrawn. He found it almost impossible to communicate what was hurting him deep-down inside. And John was very hurt.

His great love was the kitchen garden. His delight was to take me on a weekly guided tour to show me how everything was growing, or to give me his first vegetables to bring to the kitchen. When I opened the snicket gate of his garden I entered his world. In the midst of all the turmoil of running a busy conference centre these visits and time spent with him brought me peace. There on his own territory he talked to me about his life and why he was so frightened, and needed to be on his own. 'I am really frightened of people out in the world,' he said. 'The pace of life is too much for me. I am very sensitive. I don't know why, but the least thing hurts me. So this garden is my paradise. Here amongst nature I have come to life again. This walled garden is my sanctuary not my prison cell. I am really happy here; I know God listens to me. I am not escaping. I am alive here. I know God's peace in a very special way.'

After about seven years with us John was crippled by rheumatism, and could no longer work in his beloved garden. He stayed on in his little cottage until he died peacefully three years later. When he was buried in the nearby village cemetery the convent was filled to overflowing with his friends from all walks of life for his Requiem Mass, celebrated by the Bishop and many priests. It was a setting fit for a king. On his starkly plain, long coffin was a simple posy of wild flowers with the words: 'To John our gentle friend and gardener.'

John had found deep inner peace. Out in the world he knew he would lose his grip on God and that special something within himself which brought him truly deep happiness. His lifestyle was as simple as that of a child. He was one of those of whom Jesus said, 'I bless you, Father, Lord of heaven and earth for hiding these things from the learned and the clever and revealing them to children.'

Lord, teach me that people are great not because they are rich and powerful, but that in kind, gentle and ordinary people your greatness shines through to warm our lives and give us our true lasting values in life.

Contact

The good thief said: 'Jesus, remember me when you come into your kingdom.' 'Indeed, I promise you,' he replied, 'today you will be with me in paradise.' (Luke 23:42–43)

A few months ago I just managed to catch the London train for York. And as usual it was filled to overflowing, with many young people standing in the corridors. I was tired after a very busy day, and made my weary way through the different compartments hoping against hope that I might find an empty seat. No such luck until the last compartment. There I noticed a much-travelled haversack occupying precious seating accommodation.

I asked its owner politely, 'Is anyone sitting here?' knowing what a stupid question that was anyway! I was greeted by silence, and eventually a stare. My travelling companion-to-be was what is known in technical language as a 'drop out'. The sight of my clerical collar must have done for him what his dirty clothes and unkempt appearance did for me. We weren't cast in the role of ideal travelling companions. After a suitable pause when he probably wished I would go away, he got to his feet slowly, and threw his haversack onto the luggage rack in the corridor. I sat down beside him, and thanked him for his efforts. There was no response.

I made a few more efforts to talk with him, offered him my newspaper, but it was obvious he wanted nothing to do with me. He looked at his girlfriend in quiet despair. I had made my effort to be friendly, and was quite content to close my eyes. I was tired and put my arm on the elbow-rest between us. He promptly pushed it off. Eventually he allowed the narrowest of spaces for me to rest my arm with my elbow touching his. As the odours of stale sweat and bad breath came wafting across to me, I thought that this must have been the state the wounded Jesus was in when he hung on the cross. So I prayed for the Christ who was next to me on the train, and suddenly I experienced a deep inner peace. I could feel a warmth within me for my travelling companion. I knew that beneath the rough exterior there was something within him which was very precious. He was wounded by his world, and I felt such compassion for him that I was moved to silent tears. It was as if I had known him all my life, and that he was part of me.

My deep peace was disturbed when my friend and his companion pushed past me to leave the train at Peterborough. Then suddenly he turned back on his own, came up to me, shook my hand warmly and said, 'I want to thank you friend for sharing my journey.' He was soon lost in the crowd, his haversack on his back to complete the picture of a wanderer.

I believe that in some way, which I do not understand, my contact with him changed when I saw the wounded Christ in him. Touch has a wonderful healing power of its own. People surrounded Jesus during his lifetime to touch even the hem of his cloak. We heal each other through loving contact. I was lucky that day when the haversack reserved my seat so that I could sit next to my friend. Strange travelling companions, the hippie and the priest – it was good for us both that we shared the journey together and made contact.

Father, you chose us to live in this world, and you have arranged all our encounters, even the briefest, with those who travel life's journey with us. Teach us the value of a smile, a handshake, and all the small things which reveal our warmth and love for everyone so that they may see Christ in us as we see him in them.

Acceptance

Jesus said, 'Father, everything is possible for you. Take this cup away from me. But let it be as you, not I, would have it.' (Mark 14:36)

One of the most difficult things in life is to accept ourselves as we are, especially if we suffer some permanent physical disability. Michael is a typical example of what I mean.

Several years ago at the age of twenty-nine he contracted a rare virus which affected the base of his spine. From the waist down he was totally paralysed. Confined to a wheelchair he sighed for the old days when he was a powerful athlete. Being a very devout Christian he prayed earnestly that he would be able to walk again. He wrote to me describing what happened.

'When the virus struck,' he wrote, 'I couldn't believe it was happening to me. It was like a sick joke. It never sank into my mind that the paralysis was anything other than temporary. In the early days I would try to get out of bed in the normal way, only to find that my legs wouldn't obey my mind. I just lay there and cried my heart out. I was an unhappy and bitter man. My poor wife,

May, and my children became the target for my anger and frustration. For months I hardly ventured outside my home. I was too proud to let anyone see me the way I was. Soon I began to realize that I was wasting away deep inside.

'Then I heard of *people being healed* and I stormed heaven for an answer to my prayer, "Lord, make me walk again." I went to prayer groups twice, even three times a week, and everyone prayed over me. They lifted me out of my wheelchair time and again and encouraged me to walk, but my silly legs just wouldn't budge. I am six foot three and weigh sixteen stone, so it was a minor miracle that no one suffered a slipped disc or something on my account. Eventually I gave up the prayer groups, and became very angry with God. I went through a period of emptiness, of blackness, which affected every aspect of my life.

'Finally, as if in despair, I came to a healing session, and for the first time in years I did not wheel myself forward for healing. I just sat there and *allowed* God to have his way with me, to speak to me. Suddenly a huge weight seemed to lift off my shoulders, and I felt a peace I had not experienced since I became disabled. It flooded my whole body, and very gently tears began to flow, not of anger but of joy and release. I knew I was changed as a person, and had a new life to live. May and the children were sitting quietly behind me and they knew that something beautiful was happening to me. From then on our whole family life has changed, and there is real laughter in our home again. I shall probably never walk again, but there's lots of other things I can do, and I no longer resent my wheelchair.'

There are many Michaels in our world, people who have come to terms with their problem of multiple sclerosis. They bravely face the future with Christian courage, because they can identify with Christ on the cross. With him they rise to a new form of life in which they not only accept their situation, but use it to grow into people of peace and happiness.

God, you are a loving Father who will not cause us a needless tear. You know the right time to lift the burden that oppresses me, and so with a peaceful heart, at rest in your love for me, help me to concentrate more on your loving care rather than on my own preoccupation with physical pain and emotional disturbance. I place the present moment, as I do my whole life, in your tender care.